# 101
# Kerala
# Delicacies

# 101
# Kerala
# Delicacies

## G. Padma Vijay

Rupa & Co

Copyright © G. Padma Vijay 1998

First in Rupa Paperback 1998
Second impression 2000

Published by
**Rupa & Co**
7/16, Ansari Road, Daryaganj, New Delhi 110 002
135 South Malaka, Allahabad 211 001
P. G. Solanki Path, Lamington Road, Bombay 400 007
15 Bankim Chatterjee Street, Calcutta 700 073

ISBN 81-7167-278-7

Printed in India by
Gopsons Papers Ltd.
A-14 Sector 60
Noida 201 301

# CONTENTS

# PREFACE

*101 Kerala Delicacies* is a collection of traditional and popular dishes from different parts from the State of Kerala. Though the staple food of all South Indians is rice, Kerala cuisine is different from other South Indian States. However it is difficult to localise a dish as of a particular place in this State or as of Hindus, Muslims or Christians.

Almost all the dishes in this State, be it vegetarian, non-vegetarian, a sweet or snack has coconut as the basic ingredient. In the coastal towns, prawns and fish are used as a side dish every day. Mutton and chicken dishes are common to all non-vegetarians. However beef and pork predominates on the menu in the Christian household.

The book *101 Kerala Delicacies* gives an insight into a vegetarian and a non-vegetarian Keralite meal, which is served on a banana leaf. A complete meal consists of hot boiled rice which is consumed with ghee and pickle, appam or pappadam, curd and a variety of vegetarian dishes such as thoran (coconut based curry), theeyal (a sour gravy curry) or non-vegetarian dishes such as chemmeen curry (prawn curry), meen curry (fish curry). A festive meal, in addition to the above dishes is rounded up with a rice and coconut milk (or milk) kheer called 'pradhaman', which is also made with fruits and dal. Rice is also used to make nourishing breakfast dishes such as Idiappam, vellappam and appams. No meal in Kerala is complete without tongue-tickling chips made from Malabar plantains (raw), jackfruit and the starch rich root vegetable the Tapioca.

I am sure this book will offer a refreshing change to delight the palates of gourmets and experimenting cookery lovers with delicacies from South India.

G. PADMA VIJAY

# HELPFUL HINTS

1. Grease your palms and fingers with any cooking oil before peeling or cutting raw jackfruit or banana to prevent staining with the juice.

2. Grease your palm and fingers before cutting yam to prevent irritation. If the irritation is too much then discard the vegetable. Otherwise there will be throat irritation if the vegetable is consumed.

3. Keep the freshly grated coconut ready, just before starting the dish. Do not grate the coconut too long ahead of preparation time because it decays fast. If done, store in the refrigerator.

4. When preparing the coconut milk extract, allow the grated coconut to be in hot water for 5 minutes. This will yield good results. The coconut milk should always be freshly prepared just before preparing the dish.

5. If a recipe requires a Malabar plantain, never substitute it with other bananas.

6. Never use a wet spoon while handling pickles or chutneys.

7. For best results use measuring equipment for ingredients such as spoons and cups, rather than adding approximately.

8. Koorka root vegetable, tapioca root vegetable, vilimbipuli fruit, Malabar plantains can be obtained from any Kerala stores.

9. Though rice is the staple diet for Keralites which is served with a variety of vegetarian and non-vegetarian dishes, now chapatis have invaded the Keralite kitchens which of course can be served with endless varieties of vegetarian and non-vegetarian dishes.

# COOKING GLOSSARY

## CONDIMENTS AND SPICES

| English | Hindi | Malayalam |
|---------|-------|-----------|
| Asafoetida | Hing | Perungayam |
| Cardamom | Elaichi | Elathari |
| Chilli | Mirch | Mulaka |
| Cloves | Lavang | Karambu |
| Coriander | Dhania | Kothamalli |
| Cumin | Jira | Jeerakam |
| Fenugreek | Methi | Uluva |
| Garlic | Lassun | Velluli |
| Ginger | Adrak | Inji |
| Mace | Javithri | Jathipatri |
| Nutmeg | Jaiphal | Jathikkai |
| Oregano | Ajwain | Ayamodakam |
| Pepper | Kalimirch | Kurumulagu |
| Tamarind pulp | Imli | Puli |
| Turmeric | Haldi | Manjal |

## LEAFY VEGETABLES

| English | Hindi | Malayalam |
|---------|-------|-----------|
| Amaranth | Chaulai sag | Cheera |
| Cabbage | Bandgobi | Mutta kosi |
| Celery leaves | Shelari | Sellary |
| Colocasia leaves | Arvi ka sag | Chembaila |
| Coriander leaves | Hara dhania | Kothamalli |
| Curry leaves | Karipatha | Karivepilla |
| Fenugreek leaves | Methi sag | Uluvaila |
| Lettuce | Salad ka sag | Uvarcheera |
| Mint | Pudina | Pudina |
| Mustard leaves | Sarson ka sag | Kadugaila |

| | | |
|---|---|---|
| Radish leaves | Muli ka sag | Mullangila |
| Spinach | Palak | Vasala cheera |

## ROOTS AND TUBERS

| | | |
|---|---|---|
| Beetroot | Chukander | Beet |
| Carrot | Gajar | Karat |
| Colocasia | Arvi | Chembu |
| Lotus root | Kamal ki jadh | Tamara kizhangu |
| Mango ginger | Aam adrak | Manga inji |
| Onion (big) | Pyaz | Ulli or Savala |
| Onion (small) | Chota pyaz | Chumannulli |
| Potato | Alu | Urula kizhangu |
| Radish | Muli | Mullangi |
| Sweet potato | Shakarkandi | Madura kizhangu |
| Tapioca | Simla alu | Kappa |
| Yam | Zimikand | Chena |

## OTHER VEGETABLES

| | | |
|---|---|---|
| Ash gourd | Petha | Kumblanga or Elavai |
| Bitter gourd | Karela | Pavakka |
| Bottle gourd | Lauki | Chorakai |
| Brinjal | Baingan | Vazhuthananga |
| Broad beans | Bakla | Avarakka |
| Capsicum | Simla mirch | Undamulagu |
| Cauliflower | Phoolgobi | Kaliflower |
| Cluster beans | Guer ki phalli | Kothavaraka |
| Cucumber | Khira | Vellarika |
| Drumstick | Sahjan ki phalli | Muringakai |
| French beans | Bakla | French avaraka |
| Gherkins | Tindli | Kovakai |
| Jackfruit (raw) | Kacha kathal | Pacha chakka |
| Knol kohl | Kohirabi | Noolkol |
| Lady's finger | Bhindi | Vendakka |

| Lotus stem | Kamal gatta | Tamara thandu |
| Mango (raw) | Aam | Pacha manga |
| Papaya (raw) | Papita | Pacha omakaya |
| Parwar | Parwal | Potalam |
| Peas | Mattar | Pattani |
| Plantain (raw) | Kacha kela | Vazhakka |
| Plantain stem | Kela ka tana | Vazhapindi or |
| | | Vazhakambu |
| Pumpkin | Kaddu | Mathannkan |
| Ridge gourd | Tori | Peechingra |
| Snake gourd | Chachinda | Padavalanga |
| Round gourd | Tinda | Thinda |
| Tomato | Tamatar | Thakkali pazham |

## CEREALS

| Barley | Jau | Yavam |
| Milo | Juar | Cholam |
| Millet | Bajra | Kamboo |
| Maize | Makkai (bhutta) | Cholam |
| Ragi | Makra | Panjapullu |
| Rice (raw) | Arwa chaval | Pachari |
| Rice (parboiled) | Usna chaval | Puzhangal ari |
| Rice (beaten) | Chidwa | Avali |
| Rice (puffed) | Murmura | Pori |
| Semolina | Sooji | Rawa |
| Vermicelli | Siwain | Semiya |
| Wheat | Gehun | Gothambu |
| Wheat flour | Gehun ka atta | Gothambumavu |

## PULSES AND LEGUMES

| Bengal gram (whole) | Channa | Kadal |
| Bengal gram (split) | Channa dal | Kadala parippu |
| Bengal gram flour | Besan | Uzhunnu parippu |

| Cow peas | Lobia | Payar |
| Field beans | Val | Val avara |
| Green gram (whole) | Moong | Cheru payar |
| Green gram (split) | Moong dal | Cheru payar parippu |
| Horse gram | Kulthi | Muthira |
| Kesari (split) | Kesari dal | Vattu parippu |
| Lentil | Masoor dal | Masur parippu |
| Peas | Mattar | Pattani |
| Kidney beans | Rajmah | - |
| Red gram (split) | Arhar dal | Tuvara parippu |
| Soya beans | Bhatmas | Soyabeans |

## FRUITS

| Apple | Seb | Apple |
| Banana (ripe) | Kela | Vaza pazham |
| Bimbli | - | Vilimbipuli |
| Breadfruit | Madar | Kada chakka |
| Cashewfruit | Kajuphal | Kasu manga |
| Custard apple | Sharifa | Seetha pazham |
| Dates | Khajur | Eetha pazham |
| Fig | Anjeer | Atti pazham |
| Grape | Angoor | Mundi ringa |
| Jackfruit (ripe) | Kathal | Chakka |
| Jambu fruit | Jamun | Naga pazham |
| Lemon | Bara nimbu | Poonaranga |
| Lime | Nimbu | Cheru pazham |
| Mango (ripe) | Aam | Manga pazham or Pazhamanga |
| Papaya (ripe) | Papitha | Omakai |
| Peaches | Arhoo | Peaches pazham |
| Pears | Nashpati | Sabariil |
| Pineapple | Ananas | Kayitha chakka |
| Pomegranate | Anar | Mathalam pazham |

| Raisins | Kishmish | Mundiringa |
| Sapota | Sapota | Sapota |
| Wood apple | Kaith | Vilam pazham |

## NUTS AND OIL SEEDS

| Almond | Badam | Badam |
| Cashewnut | Kaju | Parangiyandi |
| Coconut | Nariyal | Thenga |
| Groundnut | Moong phali | Nelakkadala |
| Linseed seeds | Alsi | Cheru chana vithu |
| Mustard seeds | Rai | Kadugu |
| Pistachio nuts | Pista | Pista |
| Sesame seeds | Til | Ellu |
| Sunflower seeds | Surya mukhi | Surya kanthi |
| Walnut | Akhroot | Akrotandi |

## MILK AND MILK PRODUCTS

| Milk (buffalo) | Bhains ka doodh | Erumai pal |
| Milk (cow's) | Gai ka doodh | Pasum pal |
| Curd | Dahi | Thayir |
| Buttermilk | Lassi | Moru |
| Cheese | Paneer | Palkatti |
| Khoa (mawa) | Khoa | Khoa |
| Butter | Makhan | Venna |
| Ghee | Ghee | Ney |

## OTHER FOODS

| Cooking oil (vegetable) | Tel | Enna |
| Coconut milk | Nariyal ka doodh | Thenga pal |
| Coconut water | Nariyal ka pani | Thenga vellam |
| Honey | Shahad | Then |
| Jackfruit seeds | Kathal ka beej | Chakka kuru |
| Jaggery | Gud | Vellam sarkara |

| Mushroom | Tilachatto | Koon |
| Sago | Sabudana | Chauari |
| Sugarcane juice | Ganna ka ras | Karumbineeru |

## NON-VEGETARIAN FOODS

| Hen's egg | Murghi ka anda | Kozhi mutta |
| Beef | Gai ka gosht | Go mamɜam |
| Crab | Kenkra | Gnandu |
| Fowl | Murgi | Kozhi |
| Fish | Machchi | Meen or Malsium |
| Mutton | Bakhri ka gosht | Attierchi |
| Prawns | Jinga | Chemmeen |
| Pork | Suar ka gosht | Pannierchi |

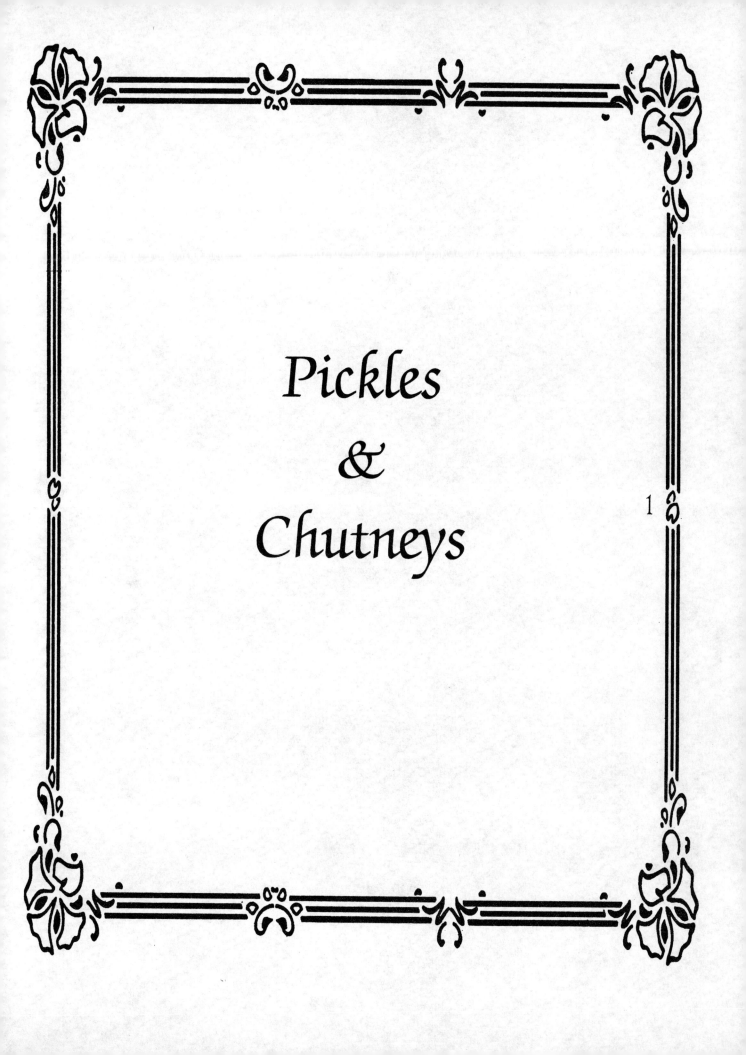

# Pickles
# &
# Chutneys

# Manga Achar

## (Plain Mango Pickle)

**Ingredients**

1 kg unripe cut mango pieces
250 gm powered salt
125 gm chilli powder
50 gm mustard seeds
50 gm fenugreek seeds
2 tsp turmeric powder
1/4 litre sesame oil

**For the seasoning**

1 tsp mustard seeds
1 tsp fenugreek seeds
1 tsp asafoetida

**Method**

1.  Roast the mustard, fenugreek seeds and powder.

2.  Wipe the mango pieces with a dry cloth.

3.  Mix the salt, chilli and roasted turmeric powder to the mango pieces in a dry plate till well mixed.

4.  Heat oil and saute the seasoning ingredients. Cool and pour over the mango mixture. Mix the contents thoroughly and store in an air-tight sterile jar.

5.  After three days, stir the contents well with a dry spoon.

6.  The pickle can be consumed after a week from the day of preparation.

7.  It is not necessary to add any preservative to the pickle nor is it essential to keep it in the sunlight and can be stored upto a period of two years.

8.  The pickle is best served with hot rice and ghee or oil spooned over it.

3

# Manga-Inji-Velluli Achar

## (Flavoury Mango Pickle)

### Ingredients

1 kg unripe mango pieces cut in small pieces
250 gm powdered salt
125 gm chilli powder
50 gm mustard seeds
25 gm fenugreek seeds
100 gm ginger
100 gm garlic
100 gm green chillies, slit lengthwise
2 tsp turmeric powder
1/4 litre sesame oil

### For the seasoning

1 tsp mustard seeds
1/2 tsp fenugreek seeds
2 tsp curry leaves

### Method

1. Roast the mustard and the fenugreek seeds and grind them to a fine powder.

2. Clean ginger and garlic and grind to a fine paste.

3. Clean the mango pieces with a dry cloth fill absolutely moisture free.

4. Mix the mango pieces with the salt, chilli powder, roasted powder and turmeric powder till well combined in a dry plate.

5. Mix the ginger-garlic paste and the slit green chillies in a plate.

6. Heat oil and saute the seasoning ingredients. Pour it over the masala paste.

7. When cool, mix the masala paste and the mango mixture till well combined.

4

8.   Store it in an air-tight sterile jar.

9.   After three days, stir the contents with a dry spoon.

10.   The pickle can be consumed after a week, from the day of preparation.

11.   It is not necessary to add any preservative to the pickle nor it is essential to keep the pickle in the sunlight and can be consumed upto a period of one year.

12.   The pickle is best served with hot rice along with ghee or oil spooned over it.

# Nellikai Achar

## (Plain Gooseberry Pickle)

**Ingredients**
1 kg goodsberry
250 gm powdered salt
125 gm chilli powder
1 tsp turmeric powder
1/4 litre sesame oil

**For the seasoning**
1 tsp mustard seeds
1 tsp fenugreek seeds
1 tsp asafoetida

## Method

1. Wash, wipe dry and remove the seeds from the gooseberries.

2. Make slits in the gooseberries with the fork.

3. Mix the gooseberries, salt, chilli powder, turmeric powder in a dry vessel till well combined.

4. Heat oil and saute the seasoning ingredients. Cool and pour over the gooseberry mixture. Mix the contents thoroughly and store it in an air-tight sterile jar.

5. Stir the contents after three days with a dry spoon.

6. The pickle can be consumed after seven days from the day of preparation.

7. It is not necessary to add any preservative nor it is essential to keep the pickle in the sunlight and can be preserved upto a period of one year.

8. It is served with hot rice with ghee or oil spooned over it.

# Nellikai-Inji-Velluli Achar

## (Flavoury Gooseberry Pickle)

**Ingredients**

1 kg gooseberry
250 gm powdered salt
125 gm chilli powder
100 gm ginger
100 gm garlic
2 tsp turmeric powder
1 cup vinegar (is used as a preservative)
1/4 litre sesame oil

**For the seasoning**

2 tsp curry leaves
1 tsp mustard seeds
1 tsp fenugreek seeds
1 tsp cumin seeds
1 tsp asafoetida

**Method**

1. Wash, wipe and remove the seeds and cut the gooseberries into pieces.

2. Mix the gooseberry pieces, salt, chilli and turmeric powder to the mango pieces and mix well. Store it in an air-tight sterile jar for 2 days.

3. Clean and grind the ginger and garlic to a fine paste.

4. Heat oil and saute and seasoning ingredients.

5. Add the ground paste and saute.

6. Add the gooseberry mixture, chilli powder and vinegar. Mix the contents thoroughly and cook for 5 minutes. Remove it from the fire and cool it.

7. Store the pickle in an air-tight sterile jar.

8. The pickle can be consumed immediately and can be preserved for one year. It is usually seemed with a hot meal and rice with ghee or oil spooned over it.

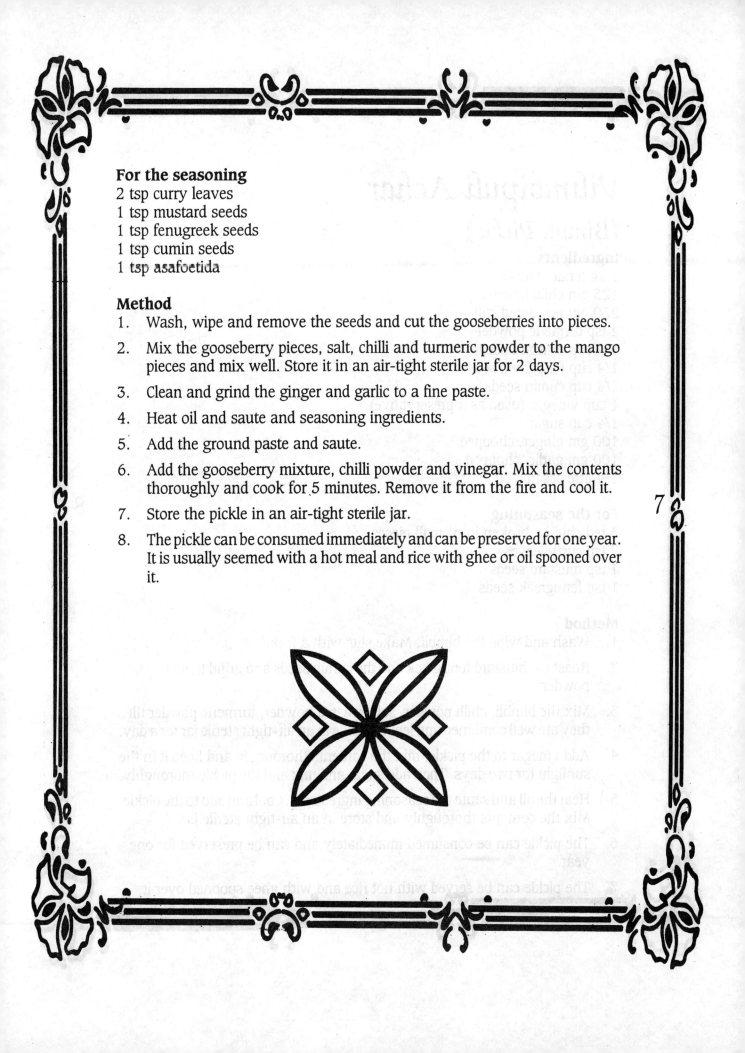

# Vilimbipuli Achar

## (Bimbli Pickle)

### Ingredients
1 kg tender bimbli
125 gm chilli powder
250 gm powdered salt
2 tsp turmeric powder
1/4 cup mustard seeds
1/4 cup fenugreek seeds
1/4 cup cumin seeds
1 cup vinegar (used as a preservative)
1/4 cup sugar
100 gm ginger, chopped
100 gm garlic, chopped
1/4 litre sesame oil

### For the seasoning
3 red chillies, broken into small pieces.
2 tsp curry leaves
1 tsp mustard seeds
1 tsp fenugreek seeds

### Method
1. Wash and wipe the bimbli. Make slits with a fork.

2. Roast the mustard fenugreek and the cumin seeds and grind them to a fine powder.

3. Mix the bimbli, chilli powder, salt, roasted powder, turmeric powder till they are well combined and leave it aside in an air-tight sterile jar for a day.

4. Add vinegar to the pickle, mix the contents thoroughly and keep it in the sunlight for two days. Then add sugar and mix and the pickle thoroughly.

5. Heat the oil and saute the seasoning ingredients. Cool and add to the pickle. Mix the contents thoroughly and store in an air-tight sterile jar.

6. The pickle can be consumed immediately and can be preserved for one year.

7. The pickle can be served with hot rice and with ghee spooned over it.

# Inji Achar

## (Ginger Pickle)

### Ingredients
250 gm ginger
1/2 cup vinegar (used a preservative)
1/2 cup dry grated coconut
2 onions
2 tsp chilli powder
2 tsp jaggery crumbled
2 tsp turmeric powder
2 tps salt

### For the seasoning
1/2 tsp mustard seeds
1/2 tsp fenugreek seeds
1/2 tsp asafoetida

### Method
1. Heat 2 tsp and saute the seasoning ingredients.

2. Warm the remaining quantity of oil and add the chilli and turmeric powder.

3. In the meantime clean and peel and ginger.

4. Grind the ginger, coconut, onions, jaggery, salt and the fried ingredients to a smooth paste.

5. Mix the ground paste with the remaining quantity of warmed up oil and the vinegar till well combined.

6. Store the pickle in an air-tight sterile jar.

7. The ginger pickle can be preserved for 6 months and can be consumed almost immediately.

8. It is usually served with hot rice along with ghee or oil spooned over it.

9

# Cheru Naranga-Inji-Velluli Achar
## (Flavoury Lime Pickle)

**Ingredients**

1 kg lime pieces
250 gm powdered salt
125 gm chilli powder
2 tsp turmeric powder
100 gm ginger
100 gm garlic
2 tsp green chillies
2 tsp mustard seeds
2 tsp fenugreek seeds
1/2 cup vinegar (used as a preservative)
1/4 litre sesame oil

**For the seasoning**

1/2 tsp mustard seeds
1/2 tsp fenugreek seeds

**Method**

1. Mix the lime pieces, salt and the turmeric powder till well combined and store in an air-tight sterile jar for two days.

2. Roast the mustard and the fenugreek seeds and grind to a fine powder.

3. Clean and grind the ginger and garlic to a fine paste.

4. Slit the green chillies lengthwise.

5. Heat oil and saute the seasoning ingredients, ground paste and the green chillies, for a minute.

6. Add vinegar, roasted powder and chilli powder and mix well.

7. Cool and pour over the lime pieces. Mix the contents thoroughly.

8. The pickle can be consumed immediately.

9. The pickle can be stored for a period of one year.

# Chemmeen Achar

## (Prawn Pickle)

### Ingredients
250 gm prawns, shelled and de-veined
100 gm ginger
100 gm garlic
4 tsp chilli powder
4 tsp salt
1/2 tsp turmeric powder
1 tsp jaggery, crumbled
1/2 cup vinegar (used as a preservative)
1/4 litre sesame oil

### For the seasoning
1/2 tsp mustard seeds
1/2 tsp fenugreek seeds
1/4 tsp asafoetida

### Method
1. Apply 2 tsp salt to prawns and allow to marinate for two hours.

2. Clean and grind the ginger and garlic to a fine paste.

3. Heat oil and fry the prawns till tender. Drain well.

4. Heat the same oil and saute the seasoning ingredients and the ground paste for a minute and cool.

5. Now mix the sauted ingredients, chilli powder, vinegar, turmeric powder, jaggery, remaining quantity of salt and the fried prawns till well combined. Cool and store in an air-tight sterile jar or bottle.

6. The prawn pickle can be consumed almost immediately.

7. This pickle is best served with hot rice with ghee or oil spooned over it.

# Meen Achar

## (Fish Pickle)

### Ingredients
500 gm pearl spot fish (Karimeen)
125 gm chilli powder
125 gm salt
1 tsp black pepper powder
1 tsp turmeric powder
50 gm ginger, cleaned and minced
50 gm garlic, minced
6 green chillies, slit lengthwise
2 tsp curry leaves
1/2 cup vinegar (used as a preservative)
1/4 litre sesame oil

### Method
1. Wash, clean and cut the fish into small pieces.

2. Mix 1 tsp chilli powder, 1 tsp salt, turmeric powder and the pepper powder till well combined.

3. Apply the mixture to fish pieces and allow it to marinate for two hours.

4. Heat the oil and fry the fish pieces till tender and drain.

5. In the same oil saute the minced ginger, garlic, green chillies and the curry leaves.

6. When cool, mix it with the remaining quantity of chilli powder, salt, vinegar and the fried fish pieces till well combined. Store it in an air-tight sterile jar.

7. This pickle can be consumed immediately and can be preserved for six months.

12

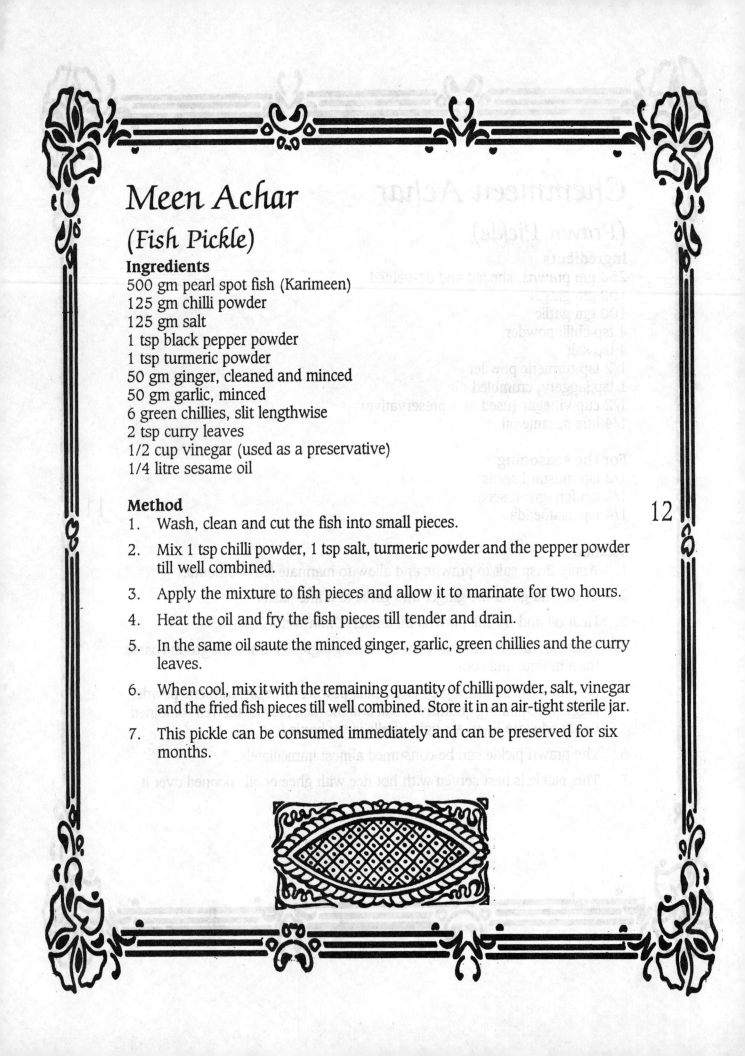

# Thenga Sambandhi

## (Coconut Chutney)

### Ingredients
1 cup freshly grated coconut
10 small Madras sambhar onions, peeled and sliced
2" piece ginger
1 tsp salt

### For the seasoning
2 tsp coconut oil
2 red chillies
2 green chillies
1/2 tsp mustard seeds

### Method
1.  Heat oil and saute the seasoning ingredients and the sliced onions.
2.  Grind the sauted ingredients, grated coconut, ginger and salt to a fine paste.
3.  This chutney can be preserved for two days only and can be served with any snack or hot rice.

13

# Manga Pullesseri

## (Curd based Mango Chutney)

### Ingredients
4 Chandrakkaran mangoes (small orange flashed mangoes), peeled
2 cups curd
1 cup freshly grated coconut
1 tsp cumin seeds
1 tsp green chilli paste
1/2 tsp salt

**For the seasoning**
4 tsp coconut oil
2 red chillies, broken into bits
2 tsp curry leaves
1/2 tsp mustard seeds

**Method**
1. Mix the grated coconut, curd and the green chilli paste till well combined. Cook on slow fire till the raw smell disappears.

2. Add mangoes, salt and boil the contents for about five minutes.

3. Heat 2 tsp coconut oil and saute the seasoning ingredients.

4. Pour it over the mango mixture.

5. Remove the mango chutney from fire and add to it the remaining quantity of coconut oil.

6. The chutney can be preserved for a week and can be served with any snack or with rice.

# Mulka Pachadi

## (Sweet-n-Sour Green Chilli Chutney)

**Ingredients**
100 gm green chillies
1 cup sesame seeds
1 cup jaggery, crumbled
1 cup tamarind pulp

1 tsp chilli powder
1/4 tsp turmeric powder
2 tsp salt
1/2 cup sesame oil

**For the seasoning**
1/2 tsp mustard seeds
1/2 tsp fenugreek seeds

**For the garnishing**
2 tsp coriander leaves, chopped

**Method**
1. Wash and wipe the green chillies. Slit them lengthwise.
2. Roast the sesame seeds and powder them.
3. Dissolve the jaggery in the tamarind pulp.
4. Add the chilli powder, turmeric powder and salt to the tarmind pulp. Boil the contents for about five minutes.
5. Heat 2 tsp oil and saute the seasoning ingredients. Add to the tamarind mixture.
6. Heat the remaining quantity of oil and fry the green chillies till tender. Add it along with the oil to the tamarind mixture. Mix the contents thoroughly till well combined.
7. Garnish the chutney with chopped coriander leaves.

15

# Vellarika Pachadi

## (Curd based Yellow Cucumber Chutney)

### Ingredients
500 gm yellow cucumber
1/2 coconut
5 green chillies
1 tsp mustard seeds
1" piece ginger
1 cup curd
1 tsp salt

### For the seasoning
4 tsp coconut oil
2 red chillies, broken into bits
2 tsp curry leaves
1/2 tsp mustard seeds

### For the garnishing
2 tsp coriander leaves, chopped

### Method
1. Wash, peel and chop the cucumber.

2. Grind the coconut, green chillies, mustard and the ginger to a fine paste.

3. Cook the cucumber with salt till just tender.

4. Add the ground paste, curd and mix the contents well. Cook further for five more minutes. Remove it from fire and transfer the contents to a serving dish.

5. Heat oil and saute the seasoning ingredients. Pour it over the cucumber chutney and mix well.

6. Garnish the chutney with the chopped coriander leaves.

7. The chutney can be consumed upto three days.

8. Serve with any snack or hot rice.

# Vegetarian
# Dishes

17

# Avial

## (Curd based Mixed Vegetable Curry)

### Ingredients
200 gm red pumpkin
200 gm ashgourd
200 gm suran (yam)
200 gm french beans
2-3 drumsticks
2-3 potatoes
2 raw bananas
1 coconut, grated
3 cups curd
5 green chillies
1 tsp cumin seeds
1/2 cup coconut oil
1 1/2 tsp salt

### For the seasoning
2 tsp curry leaves
1/2 tsp mustard seeds

### For the garnishing
2 tsp coriander leaves, chopped
2 tsp mint leaves, chopped

### Method

1. Wash, peel and cut all the vegetables into 1" pieces.

2. Cook the vegetables with 1 tsp salt and enough water till tender and dry.

3. Grind the coconut, green chillies and cumin seeds to a fine paste.

4. Mix the curd, ground paste with the remaining quantity of salt till well combined.

5. Heat 2 tsp coconut oil and saute the seasoning ingredients.

6. Stir in the cooked vegetables, curd mixture and the remaining quantity of coconut oil. Cookon low heat for five minutes and remove from the fire.

7. Transfer the contents to a serving dish.

8. Garnish the dish with chopped coriander and the mint leaves.

9. Serve accompaniment at lunch or dinner.

# Kalan

## (Curd based Raw Banana and Yam Curry)

### Ingredients
3 raw  bananas
250 gm yam (suran)
1 cup freshly grated coconut
4 green chillies
2 onions, peeled
1 tsp cumin seeds
4 red chillies
1/4 tsp turmeric powder
3 cups curd
1 tsp salt

### For the seasoning
4 tsp coconut oil
1/2 tsp mustard seeds
2 tsp curry leaves
1/4 tsp fenugreek seeds

**For the garnishing**
2 tsp fried coconut strips
2 tsp coriander leaves, chopped

**Method**
1. Wash, peel and cut the bananas and the yam into cubes.

2. Cook the vegetables with half the quantity of salt, turmeric powder and enough water till tender and dry.

3. Grind the coconut, green chillies, onions and cumin seeds to a fine paste.

4. Roast the red chillies and powder.

5. Heat oil and saute the seasoning ingredients and the ground paste for a minute.

6. Add the cooked vegetables, chilli powder, curd and the remaining quantity of salt. Mix the contents thoroughly and cook for five minutes. Remove from fire and transfer the contents to a serving dish.

7. Garnish it with the fried coconut strips and the chopped coriander leaves.

8. Serve hot with rice with ghee spooned over it.

# Olan

## (Coconut based Red Pumpkin and Beans Curry)

**Ingredients**
250 gm red pumpkin (or ashgourd)
250 gm beans
1 cup thick coconut milk (first extract)
1 tsp salt

21

**For the seasoning**
4 tsp coconut oil
2 tsp curry leaves
1/2 tsp mustard seeds
2 green chillies, minced

**For the garnishing**
2 tsp grated and roasted coconut

**Method**
1. Wash, remove the strings and cut the beans into one inch pieces.

2. Wash, peel and cut the pumkin into one inch pieces.

3. Cook the vegetables with salt and enough water till tender and dry. Transfer the contents to a serving dish.

4. Add coconut milk and stir the contents.

5. Spoon half the quantity of the coconut oil over the dish.

6. Heat the remaining quantity of coconut oil and saute the seasoning ingredients. Pour it over the curry, and mix well.

7. Garnish it with the roasted coconut.

8. Serve hot with rice.

22

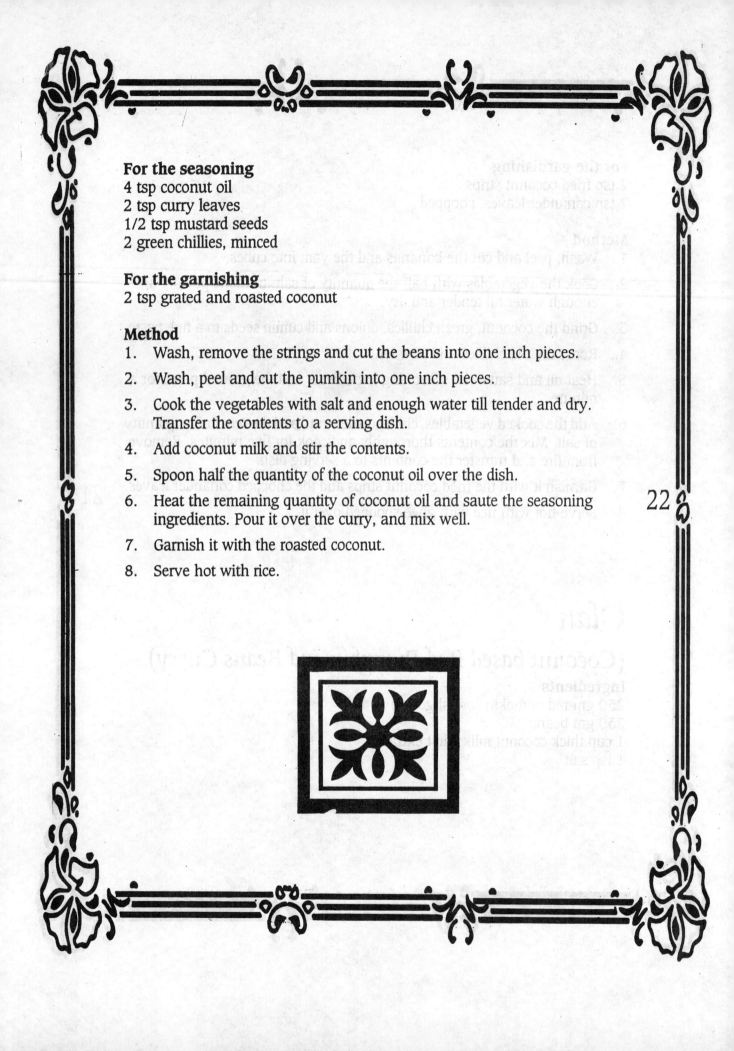

# Urla Kizhangu Curry

## (Potato Curry)

### Ingredients
500 gm medium sized potatoes
1 tsp salt

### For the gravy
1 cup freshly grated coconut
1 cup small Madras sambhar onions, peeled
2 cups coconut milk (first extract)
4 red chillies
2 tsp coriander seeds
1/2 tsp pepper
1/2 tsp cumin seeds

### For the seasoning
4 tsp coconut oil
1/2 tsp mustard seeds
2 tsp curry leaves

### For the garnishing
2 tsp chopped (mixed) nuts, fried.

### Method
1. Wash, peel and cut the potatoes into cubes.

2. Cook the potatoes with half the quantity of salt and enough water till tender and dry.

3. Roast the red chillies, coriander seeds, pepper and the cumin and powder.

4. Grind the coconut and the onions to a fine paste.

5. Heat oil and saute the seasoning ingredients and the ground paste for a minute.

6. Add coconut milk, roasted powder and the remaining quantity of salt. Cook for ten minutes.

7. Add the cooked potatoes, mix the contents thoroughly and cook for 2 more minutes. Remove it from fire and transfer the contents to a serving dish.

8. Garnish it with fried nuts.

9. Serve with any appam snacks or hot rice.

# Payar-Thenga Curry

## (Dal-n-Coconut Curry)

**Ingredients**

1/2 cup mung dal
1/2 cup tur dal
1 cup small Madras sambhar onion, peeled and sliced
1 cup coconut slices
1 tsp chilli powder
1/4 tsp turmeric powder
A pinch of asafoetida
4 green chillies
1" piece ginger
5 flakes garlic
1 tsp salt

**For the seasoning**
4 tsp coconut oil
2 tsp curry leaves
2 red chillies, broken into bits
1/2 tsp mustard seeds

**For the garnishing**
2 tsp coriander leaves, chopped

**Method**
1. Grind the green chillies, garlic and the ginger to a fine paste.
2. Mix the dals, sliced onions, coconut slices, chilli powder, turmeric powder asafoetida, ground paste salt with enough water till well combined. Pressure cook.
3. Heat oil and saute the seasoning ingredients.
4. Add the cooked dal mixture, mix the contents and cook for five minutes.
5. Remove it from fire and transfer the contents to a serving dish.
6. Garnish it with the chopped coriander leaves.
7. Serve hot with rice

25

# Muringakai Theeyal
## (Sour Drumstick Gravy)

**Ingredients**
4 drumsticks, cut into 1" pieces
1/4 kg small sambhar onions, peeled
1/2 coconut, grated
5 red chillies
3 tsp coriander seeds
A lemon size ball of tamarind

2 tsp jaggery, crumbled
2 tsp curry leaves
1/2 tsp cumin seeds
1/2 tsp pepper
1/4 tsp fenugreek seeds
1/4 tsp turmeric powder
1/4 tsp asafoetida
1 tsp salt
1/2 cup coconut oil

**For the seasoning**
2 red chillies, broken into bits
1/2 tsp mustard seeds

**For the garnishing**
1 tsp peanuts, roasted
1 tsp coriander leaves, chopped

**Method**

1. Soak the tamarind in 2 cups of hot water and extract the juice.

2. Roast the grated coconut till golden.

3. Roast the red chillies, coriander seeds, curry leaves, pepper, fenugreek and the cumin seeds till the raw smell disappears.

4. Grind the roasted ingredients to a smooth pate.

5. Cook the drumsticks with enough water till tender and dry.

6. Heat half the quantity of oil and saute the onions.

7. Add the ground paste, tamarind extract, turmeric powder, asafoetida, salt, jaggery and bring it to boil for serving minutes.

8. Add the cooked drumsticks and cook for two minutes. Remove it from fire and transfer the contents to a serving dish.

9. Heat the remaining quantity of coconut oil and saute the seasoning ingredients. Pour it over the theeyal. Mix well.

10. Garnish the dish with roasted peanuts and the coriander leaves.

11. Serve hot with rice.

# Pavakka Theeyal

## (Sour Bittergourd Gravy)

**Ingredients**

3 medium sized bittergourds
1/4 kg small sambhar onions, peeled
1 cup freshly grated coconut
2 tsp jaggery, crumbled
2 lemon size balls of tamarind
5 red chillies
3 tsp coriander seeds
2 tsp curry leaves
1/2 tsp black pepper
1/2 tsp cumin seeds
1/4 tsp fenugreek seeds
2 tsp sesame seeds
1/4 tsp turmeric powder
1/4 tsp asafoetida
1 tsp salt
1/2 cup coconut oil

**For the seasoning**

1 tsp curry leaves
1/2 tsp mustard seeds
2 red chillies, broken into bits

**For the garnishing**

1 tsp mint leaves, chopped
1 tsp coriander leaves, chopped

**Method**

1. Wash, peel and cut the bittergourds into one inch pieces.

2. Roast the grated coconut till golden.

3. Roast the red chillies, coriander seeds, curry leaves, pepper, cumin, fenugreek and the sesame seeds till the raw smell disappears.

4. Grind the roasted ingredients to a fine paste.

5. Soak the tamarind in two cups hot water, and extract the juice.

6. Cook the bittergourds till tender and dry in enough water.

7. Heat half the quantity of oil and saute the onions.

8. Add the tamarind juice, ground paste, jagger, turmeric powder, asafoetida and salt. Bring it to boil for five minutes.

9. Add the cooked bittergourds and cook for two minutes. Remove it from fire and transfer the contents to a serving dish.

10. Heat the remaining quantity of coconut oil and saute the seasoning ingredients. Pour it over the theeyal and mix.

11. Garnish the dish with the chopped mint and the coriander leaves.

12. Serve hot with rice.

# Sudevan

## (Raw Malabar Plantain Curry)

**Ingredients**
2 large raw Malabar plantains
1 cup freshly grated coconut
5 red chillies, broken into bits
3 green chillies
1 tsp jaggery, crumbled
1 tsp salt
2 cups curd
1 cup coconut oil

**For the seasoning**
2 tsp curry leaves
1/2 tsp mustard seeds
1/2 tsp cumin seeds

**For the garnishing**
2 tsp fried coconut strips
2 tsp coriander leaves, chopped

**Method**

1. Heat 1 tsp coconut oil and fry the red chillies and coarsely powder.

2. Wash, peel and cut the plantain into cubes.

3. Heat oil and fry the plantain cubes till crisp. Drain well.

4. Grind the coconut and the green chillies to a fine paste.

5. Mix the ground paste, jaggery and salt till well combined in a vessel and cook for five minutes.

6. Add curd, chilli powder and cook for five more minutes. Remove it from fire and transfer the contents to a serving dish.

7. Add the fried banana cubes to the curd mixture and mix well.

8. Heat 2 tsp coconut oil and saute the seasoning ingredients. Pour over the curry. Mix well.

9. Garnish the dish with chopped coriander leaves and the fried coconut strips.

10. Serve with rice.

# Kappa Thoran

## (Coconut based Tapioca Curry)

**Ingredients**
4 medium sized tapioca
1 cup freshly grated coconut
4 flakes garlic
4 green chillies
6 small sambhar onions, peeled
1 tsp salt

**For the seasoning**
4 tsp coconut oil
1/2 tsp chana dal
1/2 tsp urad dal
2 tsp curry leaves
1/2 tsp mustard seeds

**For the garnishing**
6-8 small sambhar onions, peeled and fried
2 tsp roasted (grated) coconut

**Method**
1.  Wash, peel and chop the tapioca.

2.  Cook the tapioca with salt and enough water till just tender and dry.

3.  Grind the coconut, garlic, green chillies and the onions to a fine paste.

4.  Heat oil and saute the seasoning ingredients and the ground paste for a minute.

5.  Add the cooked tapioca, mix the contents thoroughly and cook for five more minutes. Remove it from fire and transfer the contents to a serving dish.

6.  Garnish the dish with fried onions and roasted coconut.

7.  Serve hot with rice.

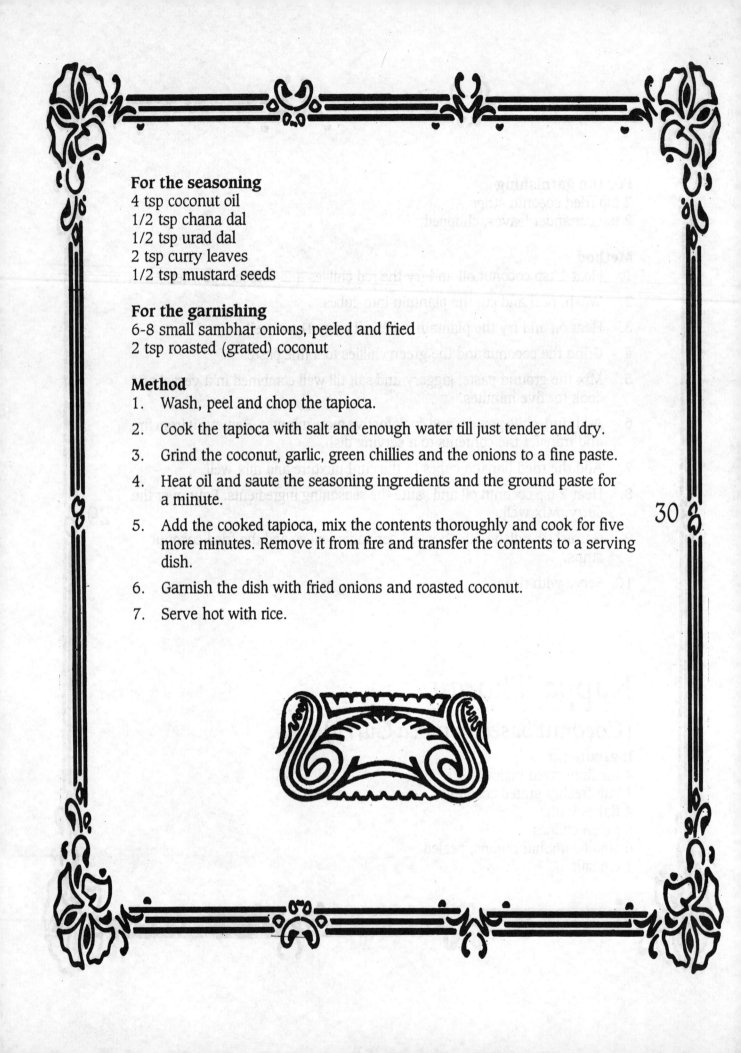

# Muttagove Thoran
## (Coconut based Cabbage Curry)

**Ingredients**

1/2 kg cabbage, finely chopped
1/2 cup freshly grated coconut
4 green chillies
4 flakes garlic
1 tsp salt
1 cup small sambhar onions, peeled and sliced

**For the seasoning**

4 tsp coconut oil
2 tsp curry leaves
1/2 tsp chana dal
1/2 tsp urad dal
1/2 tsp mustard seeds

**For the garnishing**

2 tsp freshly grated coconut
2 tsp coriander leaves, chopped

**Method**

1. Grind the coconut, green chillies and the garlic to a fine paste.

2. Heat oil and saute the seasoning ingredients, ground paste and the sliced onions for 2 minutes.

3. Add the chopped cabbage, salt and mix the contents thoroughly. Cover the pan with a lid and cook on slow fire for ten minutes till the cabbage is tender and the contents are dry. Remove it from fire and transfer the contents to a serving dish.

4. Garnish it with freshly grated coconut and the chopped coriander leaves.

5. Serve hot with rice.

# Vazhakka Ericheri

## (Raw Banana-n-Yam Curry)

### Ingredients
2 raw Malabar plantains
1/2 kg yam
2 cups freshly grated coconut
4 green chillies
1 tsp cumin seeds
1/2 tsp chilli powder
1/4 tsp turmeric powder
1 tsp salt
1/2 cup coconut oil

### For the seasoning
2 tsp curry leaves
1 tsp mustard seeds

### For the garnishing
10 small sambhar onions, peeled, sliced and fried

### Method
1. Wash, peel and cut the vegetables into cubes.

2. Mix the cubed vegetables with the chilli powder, turmeric powder, salt and enough water and cook till tender and dry.

3. Grind one cup of coconut, green chillies and the cumin seeds to a fine paste.

4. Add the ground paste to the vegetables, mix the contents and cook on slow fire further for five more minutes. Remove it from the fire and transfer the contents to a serving dish.

5. Heat one tsp of coconut oil and saute the seasoning ingredients. Pour it over the cooked vegetable.

6. Heat the remaining quantity of coconut oil and fry the remaining quantity of freshly grated coconut. Pour it over the curry and mix well.

7. Garnish the dish with the fried onions.

8. Serve hot with rice.

# Pavakka Ularthiyathu

## (Dry Bittergourd Curry)

### Ingredients
6 medium sized bittergourds
1/2 coconut, cut into thin strips
5 green chillies, slit lengthwise
1 tsp salt
1 lime

### For the seasoning
4 tsp coconut coil
1 tsp mustard seeds
2 tsp curry leaves

### For the garnishing
2 tsp grated and roasted coconut

33

### Method
1. Wash, slightly peel and scoop out the seeds from the bitter gourds. Cut the bittergourds into thin strips.

2. Mix the bittergourd strips, coconut strips, slit green chillies, salt with one cup of water and cook till tender and dry.

3. Heat oil and saute the seasoning ingredients and the cooked vegetable for 10 minutes. Remove from fire and transfer the contents to a serving dish.

4. Garnish it with roasted coconut.

5. Serve hot with rice.

# Vazhakka Payar Mizhukku Purattiyadhu

## (Raw Banana and Chauli Curry)

**Ingredients**
2 raw bananas
100 gm chauli
1/2 cup freshly grated coconut
3 green chillies
1 tsp salt

**For the seasoning**
4 tsp coconut oil
1/2 tsp mustard seeds
2 tsp curry leaves

**For the garnishing**
2 tsp coriander leaves, chopped

34

**Method**

1.  Wash, peel and cut the bananas and the chauli into one inch pieces.

2.  Cook the vegetables with salt and enough water till tender and dry.

3.  Grind the coconut and the green chillies to a fine paste.

4.  Heat oil and saute the seasoning ingredients and the ground paste for a minute. Add the cooked vegetables mix the contents thoroughly and cook for another five minutes. Remove it from fire and transfer the contents to a serving dish.

5.  Garnish the dish with the chopped coriander leaves and the mint leaves.

6.  Serve hot with rice and ghee spooned over it.

# Koorka Curry

## (Koorka Root Vegetable Curry)

### Ingredients
250 gm koorka root vegetable
1/4 tsp turmeric powder
1 cup sambhar onions, peeled and sliced
1 tsp chilli powder
1/2 tsp salt

### For the seasoning
4 tsp coconut oil
2 tsp curry leaves
1/2 tsp mustard seeds

### For the garnishing
8 tapioca chips, crushed

### Method
1. Wash and boil the vegetable with salt, turmeric powder and enough water till tender and dry. Remove the peel of the vegetable.

2. Heat oil and saute the seasoning ingredients and the sliced onions for a minute.

3. Add the cooked vegetable and the chilli powder, mix the contents thoroughly and cook for 2 more minutes. Remove it from fire and transfer the contents to a serving dish.

4. Garnish the dish with the crushed tapioca chips.

5. Serve hot with rice.

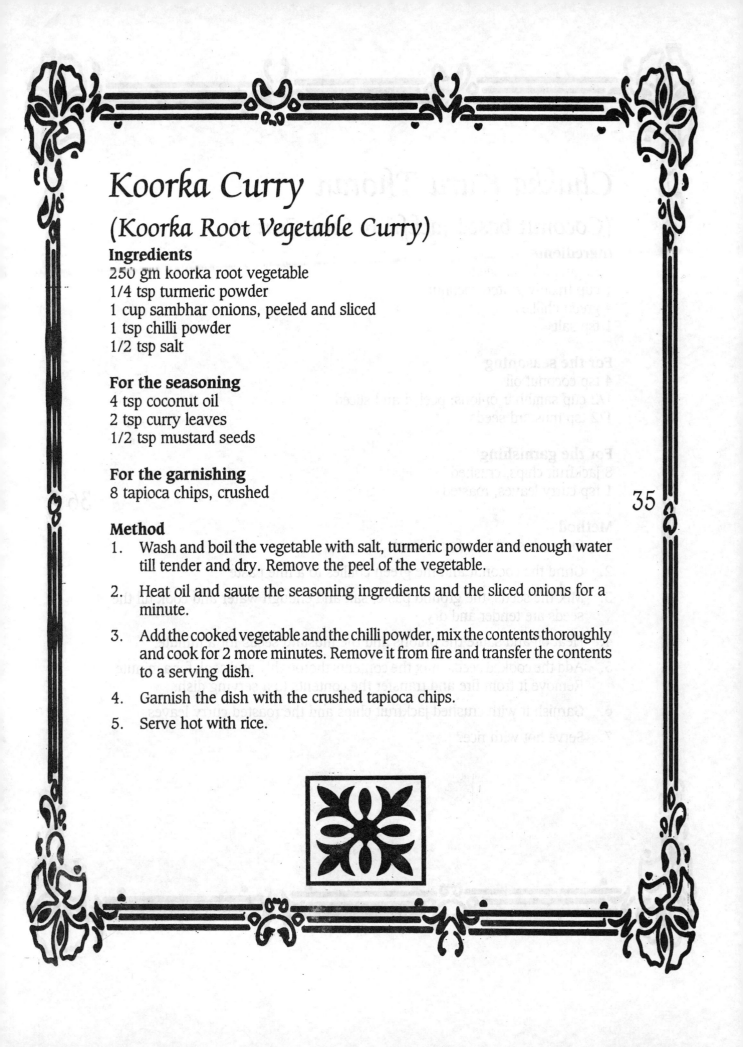

# Chakka Kuru Thoran

## (Coconut based Jackfruit Seed Curry)

### Ingredients
500 gm jackfruit seeds
1 cup freshly grated coconut
4 green chillies
1 tsp salt

### For the seasoning
4 tsp coconut oil
1/2 cup sambhar onions, peeled and sliced
1/2 tsp mustard seeds

### For the garnishing
8 jackfruit chips, crushed
1 tsp curry leaves, roasted

### Method
1.  Cut each seed into four pieces.

2.  Grind the coconut and the green chillies to a fine paste.

3.  Mix the seeds, the ground paste, salt and enough water and cook till the seeds are tender and dry.

4.  Heat oil and saute the onions and the mustard seeds for a minute.

5.  Add the cooked seeds, mix the contents thoroughly and cook for a minute. Remove it from fire and transfer the contents to a serving dish.

6.  Garnish it with crushed jackfruit chips and the roasted curry leaves.

7.  Serve hot with rice.

# Chakka Peralan

## (Jackfruit Seed Curry Kerala Style)

### Ingredients

1/2 medium sized raw jackfruit
1 cup freshly grated coconut
4 green chillies
1/2 tsp cumin seeds
1/4 tsp turmeric powder
1 tsp curry leaves

### For the seasoning

1/4 cup coconut oil
3 red chillies, broken into bits
1/2 tsp mustard seeds
2 tsp curry leaves

### For the garnishing

2 tsp chopped and fried nuts
2 tsp coriander leaves, chopped

### Method

1. Cut the soft portion of the jackfruit into small pieces

2. Cook with salt, turmeric powder and enough water till tender and mash it thoroughly.

3. Grind the coconut, green chillies and cumin seeds to a fine paste.

4. Heat oil and saute the seasoning ingredients and the ground paste for a minute.

5. Add the mashed jackfruit, mix the contents thoroughly and cook on slow fire with occasional stirring for five minutes. Remove it from the fire and transfer the contents to a serving dish.

6. Garnish it with fried nuts and chopped coriander leaves.

7. Serve hot with rice.

# Vazhakka-Koorka Upperi

## (Raw Banana and Koorka Root Vegetable Shallow Fried Curry)

### Ingredients
2 small raw bananas
250 gm koorka root vegetable
1 tsp chilli powder
1/4 tsp turmeric powder
1 tsp salt
1/2 cup coconut oil

### For the garnishing
2 tsp curry leaves, roasted
2 tsp freshly grate, coconut

### Method
1. Wash, peel and cut the bananas and the root vegetable into thin strips
2. Mix the vegetable with turmeric powder, salt and just enough water and cook till just tender and dry.
3. Heat oil in a pan and fry the vegetables on slow fire. Add chilli powder and mix the contents thoroughly. Remove it from fire and transfer the contents to a serving dish.
4. Garnish the dish with the grated coconut and the roasted curry leaves.
5. Serve hot with rice.

# Kadala Curry

## (Chana Curry)

### Ingredients
1 cup kabuli chana
1/2 cup jackfruit pieces (raw)
1 cup freshly grated coconut
1 tsp chilli powder
1/4 tsp turmeric powder
1 tsp jaggery, crumbled
1 tsp salt

### For the seasoning
4 tsp coconut oil
2 tsp curry leaves
1/2 tsp mustard seeds
1/2 tsp urad dal

### For the garnishing
2 tsp coriander leaves, chopped
2 tsp mint leaves, chopped

### Method

1. Soak the kabuli chana in water overnight.

2. Mix the kabuli chana, jackfruit pieces, chilli powder, turmeric powder and salt till well combined with enough quantity of water and pressure cook for about 12-15 minutes.

3. Grind half the quantity of coconut to a fine paste.

4. Mix the cooked chana, jackfruit, ground coconut paste and jaggery till well combined.

5. Heat oil in a pan and saute the seasoning ingredients and the remaining quantity of the grated coconut for a minute.

6. Add the cooked mixture, mix the contents thoroughly and cook for a minute more. Remove it from fire and transfer the contents to a serving dish.

7. Garnish the dish with the coriander leaves and the mint leaves.

8. Serve with hot rice and pappadam.

# Pulicherry

## (Savoury and Flavoury Buttermilk)

### Ingredients
1/2 litre buttermilk
5 small sambhar onions, peeled
4 tsp freshly grated coconut
4 flakes garlic
1 tsp cumin seeds
5 green chillies, slit lengthwise
1 tsp ginger, grated
1/4 tsp turmeric powder
1/2 tsp salt

### For the seasoning
3 tsp ghee or coconut oil
6 sambhar onions, peeled and sliced
2 tsp curry leaves
3 red chillies, broken to bits
1/2 tsp mustard seeds
1/4 tsp fenugreek seeds

### For the garnishing
2 tsp coriander leaves, chopped
2 tsp mint leaves, chopped

**Method**

1. Grind the coconut, onions, garlic and the cumin seeds to a fine paste.

2. Add the slit green chillies, grated ginger, turmeric powder to half cup of water and bring the contents to boil for 2-3 minutes.

3. Mix the buttermilk, chilli ginger water and salt till well combined.

4. Heat ghee or oil and saute the seasoning ingredients and the ground paste for a minute.

5. Pour over it the buttermilk and boil the contents for five minutes.

6. Remove it from fire and transfer the contents to a serving dish.

7. Garnish it with the chopped coriander and the mint leaves.

8. Serve with rice and pappadam.

# Kaichakka Khitchadis

## (Curd based Pineapple-n-Coconut Curry)

**Ingredients**

1 cup pineapple slices (ripe)
2 cups freshly grated coconut
1 tsp cumin seeds
1/4 tsp turmeric powder
2 cups curd
1/2 tsp salt
1/2 cup sambhar onions, peeled and sliced

**For the seasoning**

2 tsp coconut oil
1/2 tsp mustard seeds
2 red chillies, broken into bits

**For the garnishing**

2 tsp grated pineapple

2 tsp fried coconut strips

**Method**

1. Cook the pineapple with the turmeric powder and 1/2 cup of water till dry.

2. Grind the coconut and the cumin seeds to a fine paste.

3. Mix the cooked pineapple, coconut paste, curd and salt till well combined in a serving dish.

4. Heat oil and saute the seasoning ingredients and the sliced onions for a minute and pour over the pineapple mixture.

5. Garnish the dish with grated pineapple and fried coconut strips.

6. Serve with rice and pappadam.

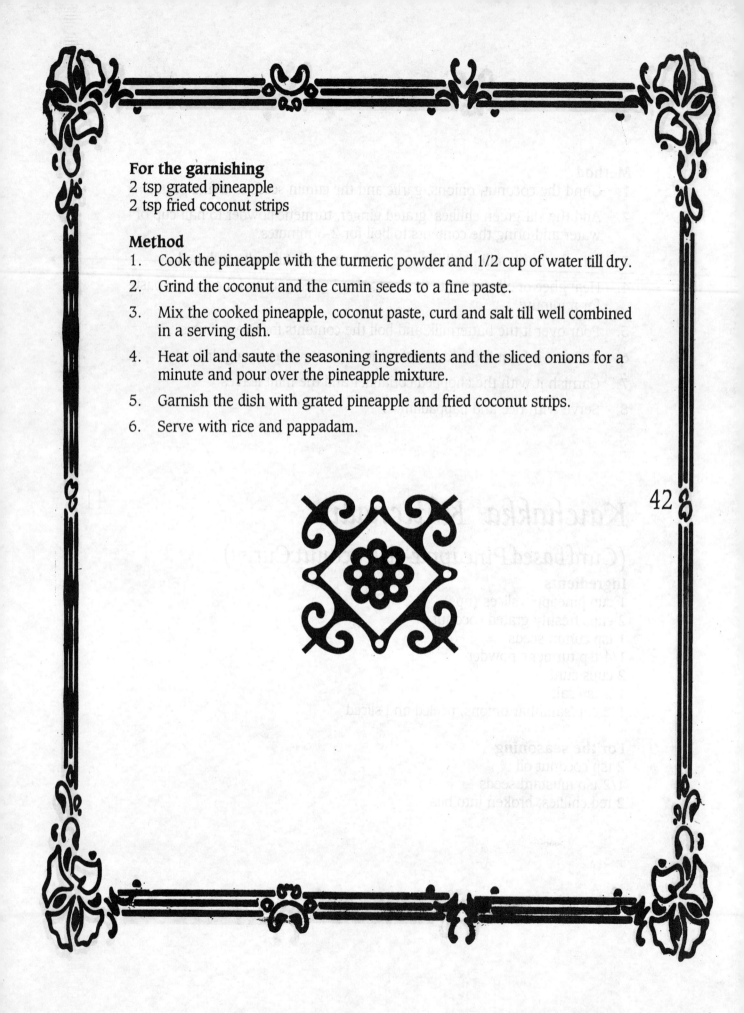

42

# Prawn
# Dishes

43

# Chemmeen Theeyal

## (Sour Prawn Gravy)

### Ingredients
250 gm prawns
1/4 kg small sambhar onions, peeled and sliced
1 cup freshly grated coconut
6 red chillies
2 tsp curry leaves
2 tsp pepper
1/2 tsp fenugreek seeds
1/2 tsp cumin seeds
1/2 tsp turmeric powder
1/4 tsp asafoetida
A lemon size ball of tamarind
1 tsp salt

### For the seasoning
4 tsp coconut oil
1/2 tsp mustard seeds
1 tsp curry leaves
2 red chillies, broken into bits

### For the garnishing
2 tsp coriander leaves, chopped
1 tsp mint leaves, roasted

### Method
1.  Soak tamarind in two cups of warm water and extract the juice.

2.  Roast the grated coconut till brown.

3.  Roast the red chillies, coriander seeds, curry leaves, pepper, fenugreek seeds and the cumin seeds.

45

4. Grind the roasted ingredients to a fine paste.

5. Wash, shell and de-vein the prawns.

6. Cook prawns and onions with enough water till tender and dry.

7. Add the ground paste, turmeric powder, asafoetida, tamarind juice and salt. Cook till the gravy is thick. Remove it from the fire and transfer the contents to a serving dish.

8. Heat oil and saute the seasoning ingredients for a minute. Pour over the prawn gravy. Mix well.

9. Garnish the dish with the chopped coriander leaves and the mint leaves.

10. Serve hot with rice and pappadam.

# Chemmeen-Vazhakka Curry
## (Prawn and Raw Banana Curry)

**Ingredients**
250 gm prawns
1/2 tsp chilli powder
1/4 tsp turmeric powder
5 green chillies, slit lengthwise
8 sambhar onions, peeled
1/2 cup freshly grated coconut
1 tsp cumin seeds
1 tsp salt

**For the seasoning**
4 tsp coconut oil
2 tsp curry leaves
1/2 tsp mustard seeds

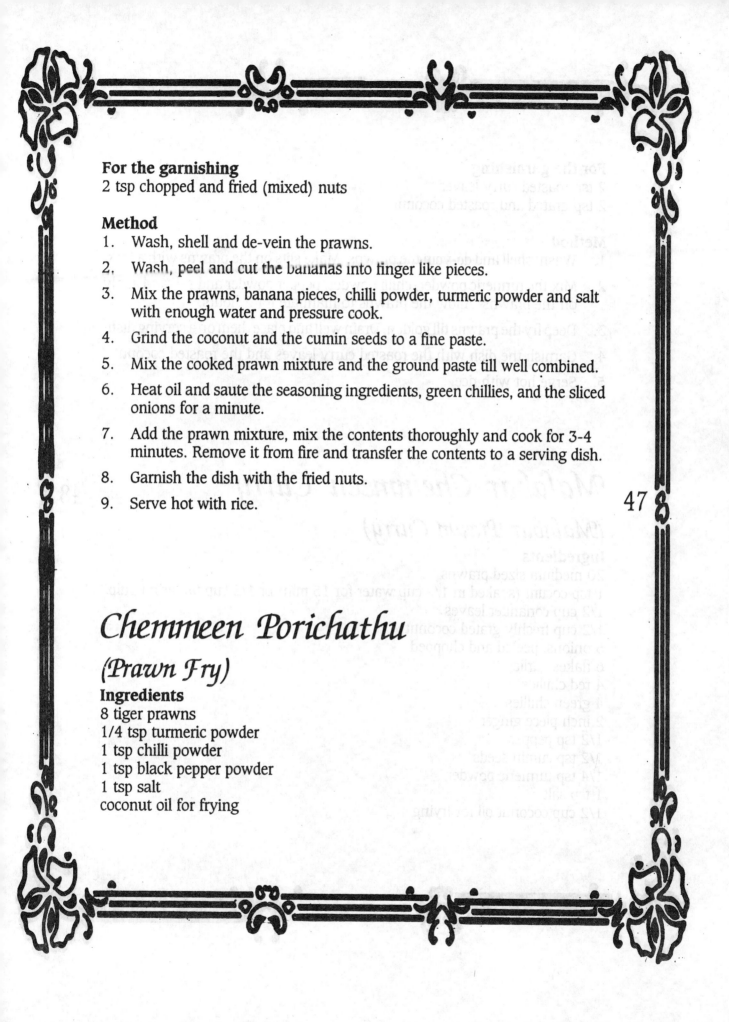

**For the garnishing**
2 tsp chopped and fried (mixed) nuts

**Method**
1.  Wash, shell and de-vein the prawns.

2.  Wash, peel and cut the bananas into finger like pieces.

3.  Mix the prawns, banana pieces, chilli powder, turmeric powder and salt with enough water and pressure cook.

4.  Grind the coconut and the cumin seeds to a fine paste.

5.  Mix the cooked prawn mixture and the ground paste till well combined.

6.  Heat oil and saute the seasoning ingredients, green chillies, and the sliced onions for a minute.

7.  Add the prawn mixture, mix the contents thoroughly and cook for 3-4 minutes. Remove it from fire and transfer the contents to a serving dish.

8.  Garnish the dish with the fried nuts.

9.  Serve hot with rice.

47

# Chemmeen Porichathu

## (Prawn Fry)
**Ingredients**
8 tiger prawns
1/4 tsp turmeric powder
1 tsp chilli powder
1 tsp black pepper powder
1 tsp salt
coconut oil for frying

**For the garnishing**
2 tsp roasted curry leaves
2 tsp grated and roasted coconut

**Method**
1. Wash, shell and de-vein the prawns. Make slits on the prawns with a fork.

2. Mix the turmeric powder, chilli powder, pepper powder and salt and apply on the prawns. Allow the prawns to marinate for 2 hours.

3. Deep fry the prawns till golden. Drain well and place them on a serving dish.

4. Garnish the dish with the roasted curry leaves and the roasted coconut.

5. Serve hot with rice.

# Malabar Chemmeen Curry

## (Malabar Prawn Curry)

**Ingredients**
20 medium sized prawns
1 tsp cocum (soaked in 1/2 cup water for 15 min) or 1/2 cup tamarind pulp
1/2 cup coriander leaves
1/2 cup freshly grated coconut
5 onions, peeled and chopped
6 flakes garlic
4 red chillies
4 green chillies
2 inch piece ginger
1/2 tsp pepper
1/2 tsp cumin seeds
1/4 tsp turmeric powder
1 tsp salt
1/2 cup coconut oil for frying

**For the garnishing**

2 tsp curry leaves, fried in oil
6 cashew nuts, chopped and fried
1/2 tsp cardamom powder

**Method**

1. Wash, shell and de-vein the prawns.

2. Grind the coriander leaves, coconut, onions, garlic, red chillies, green chillies, ginger, pepper, cumin to a fine paste.

3. Apply the paste to the prawns and allow to marinate for 2 hours.

4. Heat oil and fry the prawns till golden and drain well.

5. Mix the tamarind juice or cocum, turmeric powder and salt in a vessel.

6. Add the fried prawns and boil for five minutes. Remove it from fire and transfer the contents to a serving dish.

7. Garnish it with the fried curry leaves and the nuts. Sprinkle cardamom powder on them.

8. Serve with hot rice.

49

# Chemmeen Varthada

## (Prawn Roast)

**Ingredients**

20 tiger prawns
1 tsp mustard seeds
5 green chillies, chopped
1" piece ginger, chopped

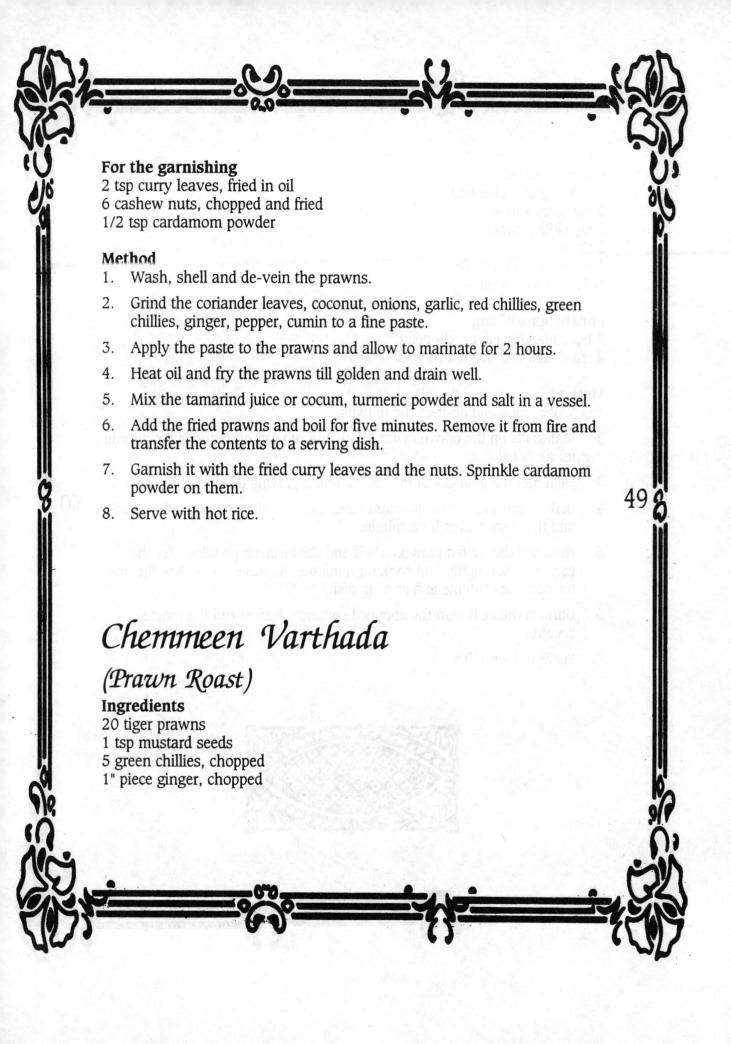

4 onions, sliced
6 flakes garlic, chopped
2 tsp curry leaves
2 tsp chilli powder
2 tsp salt
1/4 tsp turmeric powder
1/2 cup coconut oil

**For the garnishing**
2 tsp coriander leaves, chopped
2 tsp grated and roasted coconut

**Method**
1.  Wash, shell and de-vein the prawns.
2.  Make slits on the prawns with a fork and rub salt on it and leave it aside for an hour.
3.  Heat half the quantity of oil and saute the prawns till tender. Drain.
4.  In the same oil saute the mustard seeds, green chillies, ginger, onion, garlic and the curry leaves for a minute.
5.  Now add the sauted prawns, chilli and the turmeric powder. Mix the contents thoroughly and cook for a minute. Remove it from the fire and transfer the contents to a serving dish.
6.  Garnish the dish with the chopped coriander leaves and the roasted coconut.
7.  Serve hot with rice.

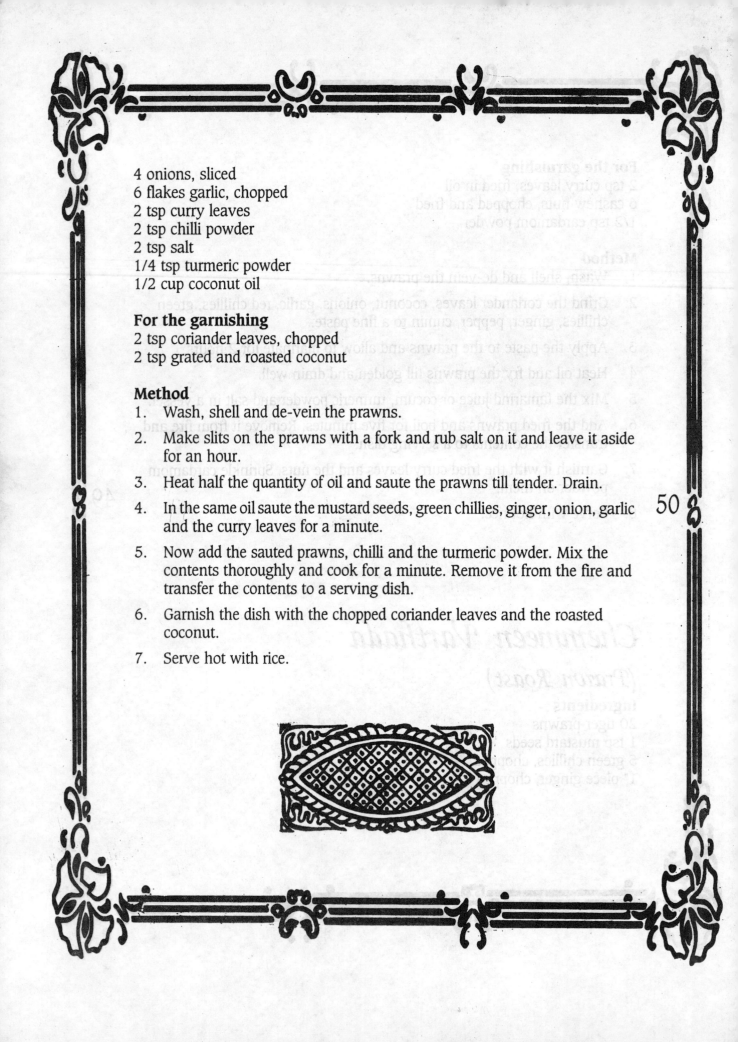

Achchappam (Rose Cookies).

Kozhierchi Curry (Chicken Curry).

Vazhakka, Chakka and Kappa Upperi (Raw Banana, Jackfruit and Tapioca Chips).

Vazahakka Pazham Uniappam (Banana and Rice Moulds).

Pappadam (Papad).

Kuzhalappam (Rice Rolls).

Idiappam (String Hoppers).

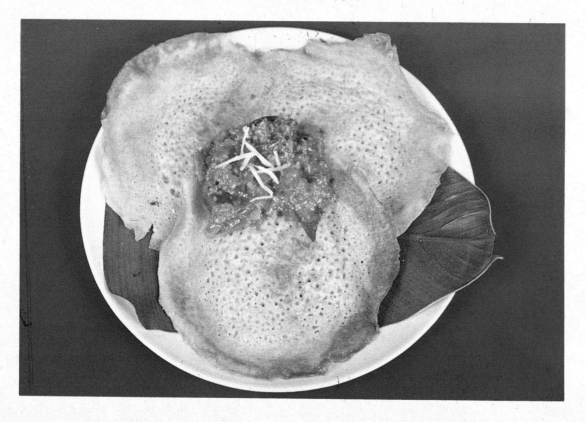

Palappam.

Puttu (Rice and Coconut Delicacy).

Vellappam (Rice Pancake).

Inji Achar (Ginger Pickle).

Avial (Curd based Mixed Vegetable Curry).

Muringakai Theeyal (Sour Drumstick Gravy).

Kootu Curry (Yam-n-raw Banana Curry).

Malabar Chemmeen Curry (Malabar Prawn Curry).

Pollicha Meen Curry (Baked Fish Curry).

# Kappa-Chemmeen Curry
## (Tapioca and Prawn Curry)

### Ingredients
8 medium sized prawns
2 medium sized tapioca
1/2 cup freshly grated coconut
1/2 cup tamarind pulp
4 onions, peeled
1/2 tps cumin seeds
1/2 tsp pepper
1" piece ginger
1/4 tsp fenugreek seeds
1 tsp salt

### For the seasoning
1/4 tsp coconut oil
2 tsp curry leaves
2 red chillies, broken into bits
1/2 tsp mustard seeds

### For the garnishing
2 tsp mint leaves, roasted
2 tsp coriander leaves, chopped

### Method
1. Grind the coconut, onions, cumin seeds, pepper, ginger and the fenugreek seeds with half the quantity of salt to a smooth paste.

2. Wash, shell and de-vein the prawns. Make slits on them with a fork.

3. Apply the ground paste on the prawns and allow them to marinate for two hours.

4. Wash, peel and chop the tapioca. Cook with the remaining quantity of salt and enough water till tender and dry.

5. Heat oil and saute the seasoning ingredients.

6. Add the prawn mixture, mix the contents thoroughly and simmer till the prawn is tender.

7. Add the tamarind pulp and the cooked tapioca. Mix the contents well and cook for five more minutes. Remove it from fire and transfer the contents to a serving dish.

8. Garnish it with the roasted mint leaves and the chopped coriander leaves.

9. Serve with hot rice.

# Chemmeen Thoran
## (Coconut based Prawn Curry)

**Ingredients**
500 gm prawns (small)
1 cup freshly grated coconut
5 green chillies, chopped
1" piece ginger, chopped
6 flakes garlic, chopped
1 tsp chilli powder
1/4 tsp turmeric powder
1 tsp salt

**For the seasoning**
4 tsp coconut oil
2 tsp curry leaves
1/2 tsp chana dal
1/2 tsp urad dal
1/2 tsp mustard seeds

**For the garnishing**

2 tsp coconut oil

2 tsp coriander leaves, chopped

**Method**

1.. Wash, shell and de-vein the prawns.

2. Cook the prawns with salt and enough quantity of water till tender and dry.

3. Heat oil and saute the seasoning ingredients and the chopped ingredients for a minute.

4. Add the cooked prawns, chilli powder, turmeric powder and the grated coconut. Mix the contents well and cook for five minutes. Remove it from fire and transfer the contents to a serving dish.

5. Garnish it with chopped coriander leaves and spoon coconut oil over it.

6. Serve hot with rice.

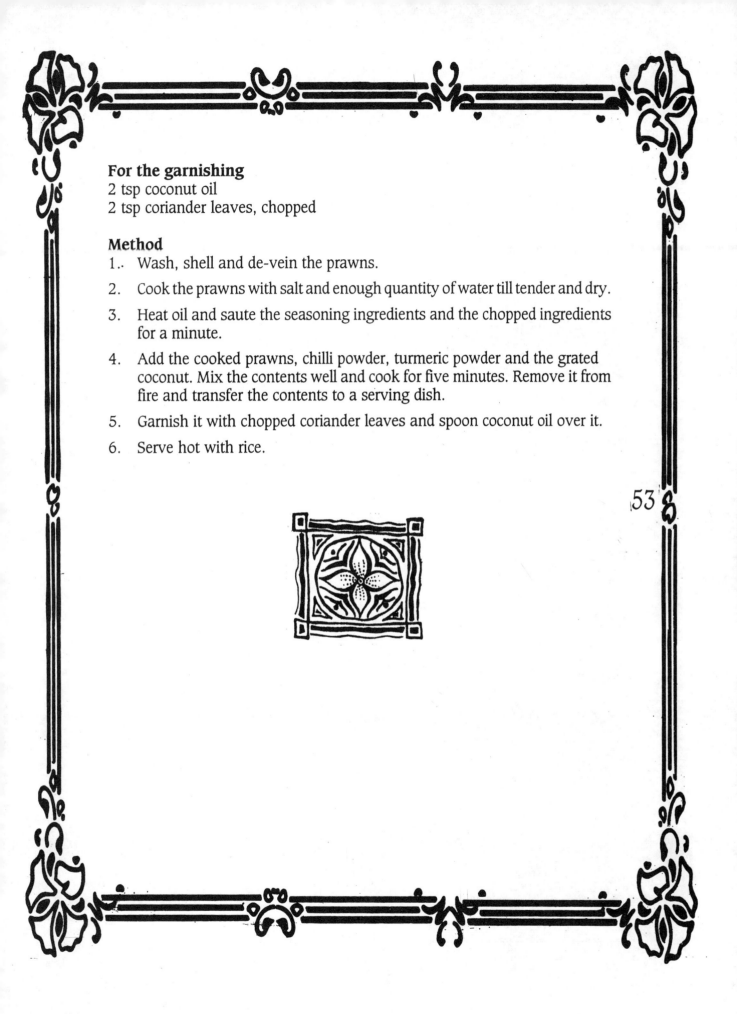

# Fish
# Dishes

55

Fish
Dishes

# Fish Stew

**Ingredients**

500 gm fish (any variety)
1 coconut, grated
1 inch ginger, minced
5 green chillies, minced
5 cloves
1" cinnamon stick
2 black cardamons
1/2 tsp pepper powder
1 tsp salt
1/2 cup coconut oil

**For the seasoning**

2 tsp curry leaves
1/2 tsp mustard seeds

**For the garnishing**

8 small sambhar onions, peeled and fried
2 tsp coconut strips, fried

**Method**

1. Clean and cut the fish into small pieces.

2. Prepare two extracts of coconut, first with 1 cup of warm water, second with 2 cups of warm water.

3. Heat oil in a pressure pan and saute the seasoning ingredients, minced ginger, chillies, cloves, cinnamon, cardamoms and the fish pieces for 2-3 minutes.

4. Add the second extract and salt and pressure cook.

5. Finally add the first extract and the pepper powder and boil it for a minute. Remove it from fire and transfer the contents to a serving dish.

6. Garnish it with the fried sambhar onions and the fried coconut strips.

7. Serve hot with appam or pappadam.

(The popular fish varieties used in Kerala are Pearl spot, black or silver Pomfrets, Mullets, Sardines, Mackerel, Salmon and Jew fish).

# Meen Porichathu

## (Fish Fry)

### Ingredients
1 pearl spot fish (karimeen)
1/4 kg small sambhar onions, peeled
3 red chillies
3 green chillies
4 flakes garlic
1" piece ginger
1/4 tsp turmeric powder
4 tsp vinegar
1 tsp salt
1 cup coconut oil

### For the garnishing
1/2 cup sambhar onions, peeled and fried
2 tsp fried coconut strips

58

### Method
1.  Wash, clean and cut the fish into 12 pieces.

2.  Grind the onions, red chillies, green chillies, garlic, ginger to a fine paste.

3.  Mix the ground paste with the turmeric powder, vinegar and salt till well combined.

4.  Apply the paste to the fish pieces and allow it to marinate for 2 hours.

5.  Heat oil and fry the pieces till golden. Drain well and place it in a serving dish.

6.  Garnish the dish with fried onions and fried coconut strips.

7.  Serve with hot rice.

# Meen Thoran

## (Coconut based Fish Curry)

### Ingredients
250 gm small variety fish
1 cup freshly grated coconut
4 green chillies
1" piece ginger
5 flakes garlic
1/2 tsp chilli powder
1/4 tsp turmeric powder
1 tsp coriander powder
1 tsp salt

### For the seasoning
4 tsp coconut oil
2 tsp curry leaves
1/2 cup chana dal
1/2 tsp urad dal
1/2 tsp mustard seeds

### For the garnishing
2 tsp fresh coconut oil
2 tsp coriander leaves, chopped

### Method
1. Wash and clean the fish.

2. Grind the coconut, chillies, ginger, garlic to a fine paste.

3. Mix the fish, chilli powder, turmeric powder, coriander powder and salt till well combined. Cook with enough water till tender and dry.

4. Heat oil and saute the seasoning ingredients for about a minute.

5. Add the cooked fish and the ground paste. Mix the contents well and cook for another five minutes. Remove from the fire and transfer the contents to a serving dish.

6. Spoon coconut oil over the dish and garnish with chopped coriander leaves.

7. Serve hot with rice.

# Keralite Syrian Meen Curry

## (Keralite Syrian Fish Curry)

### Ingredients
500 gm dried fish, cleaned
1 coconut
3 tsp coriander seeds
1 tsp pepper
8 small sambhar onions, peeled
4 red chillies
5 flakes garlic
1 cup sliced onions
2 tsp ginger, grated
5 green chillies, chopped
2 tsp vinegar
1 tsp salt
1/4 tsp coconut oil

### For the seasoning
2 tsp curry leaves
1/2 tsp mustard seeds
1/2 tsp fenugreek seeds

### For the garnishing
2 tsp grated and roasted coconut
2 tsp coriander leaves, chopped

### Method
1. Grate the coconut and prepare two extracts with the coconut, the first with 1 cup of warm water and the second with 2 cups of warm water.

2. Roast the coriander seeds, red chillies and the pepper.

3. Grind the roasted ingredients with the onion and the garlic to a fine paste.

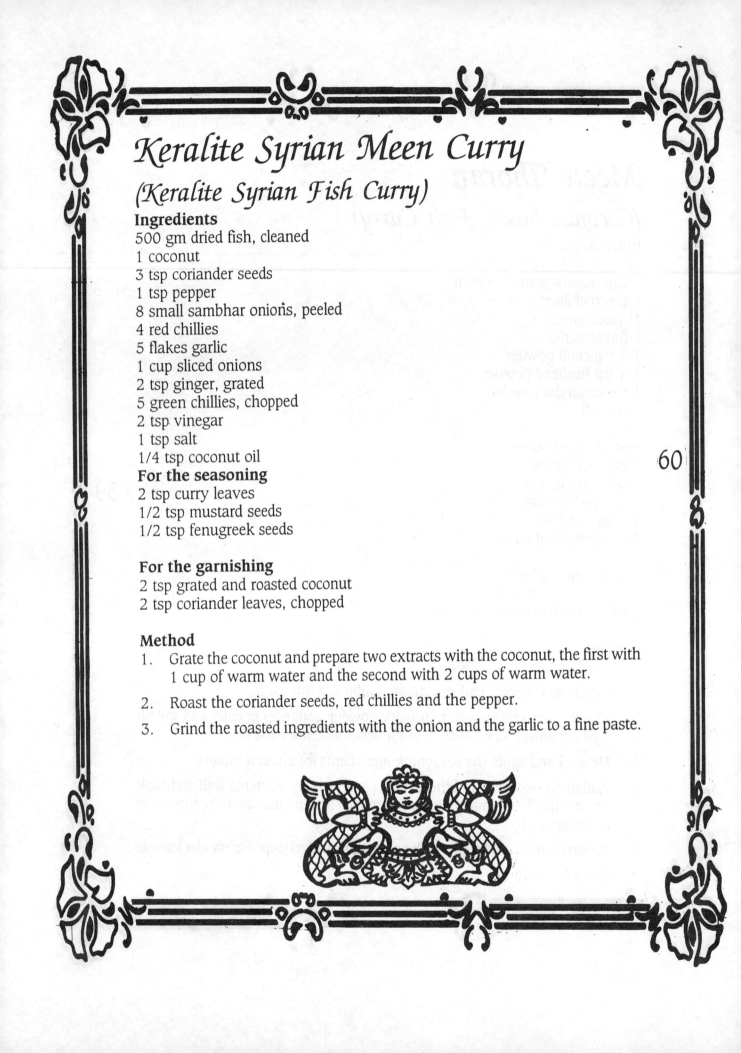

4. Heat oil and saute the seasoning ingredients and the chopped ginger, green chillies and the sliced onions for a minute.

5. Add the dried fish, vinegar, salt, ground paste along with the second coconut extract. Mix the contents thoroughly and cook till the fish is tender and the gravy is thick.

6. Add the dried extract and cook for five more minutes. Remove it from fire and transfer the contents to a serving dish.

7. Garnish it with roasted coconut and the chopped coriander leaves.

8. Serve hot with rice.

# Malabar Meen Curry

## (Malabar Fish Curry)

**Ingredients**
12 sardines, cleaned
2 cups freshly grated coconut
7 onions, sliced
1 tsp cocum (kodumpuli)
5 flakes garlic
4 green chillies
1" piece ginger
1 tomato
2 tsp coriander leaves
1 tsp salt
1/4 cup coconut oil

**For the seasoning**
2 tsp curry leaves
1/2 tsp mustard seeds

**For the garnishing**
2 tsp mint leaves, chopped

**Method**
1. Soak the cocum in 1/2 cup of water for 10 minutes.

2. Grind the coconut, cocum, onions, garlic, green chillies, ginger, tomato and the coriander leaves to a fine paste.

3. Heat half the quantity of oil in a pan and saute the seasoning ingredients and the ground paste for a minute.

4. Add fish, salt and 2 cups of water. Bring the contents to boil and cook on slow fire till the fish is tender and the contents are dry. Pour over the curry, the remaining quantity of coconut oil, mix well and remove it from the fire. Transfer the contents to a serving dish.

5. Garnish the dish with chopped mint leaves.

6. Serve hot with rice.

# Meen Vevichatu

## (Fish Curry cooked in its gravy on slow fire)

**Ingredients**
500 gm fish pieces (any variety)
2 tsp coriander powder
2 tsp chilli powder
1 cup sambhar onions, peeled
5 flakes garlic
1/2 cup cocum (kodumpuli)
2" piece ginger, chopped
1 tsp salt

**For the seasoning**
4 tsp coconut oil
2 tsp curry leaves
1/2 tsp mustard seeds
1/2 tsp fenugreek seeds

**For the garnishing**
2 tsp grated and roasted coconut
2 tsp mixed nuts, grated

## Method
1. Roast the coriander powder and the chilli powder.
2. Grind the onions and the garlic to a fine paste.
3. Soak the cocum in 2 cups of water for about 15 minutes.
4. Mix the fish pieces and the salt and allow it to marinate for 15 minutes.
5. Heat oil in a pan and saute the seasoning ingredients, ground paste and the chopped ginger for a minute.
6. Add the fish pieces, cocum water, roasted powder and mix thoroughly. Cover the pan with a lid and cook on slow fire till the fish is tender and the gravy is thick. Remove from the fire and transfer the contents to a serving dish.
7. Garnish it with roasted coconut and the grated nuts.
8. Serve hot with rice.

# Karimeen Polichathu
## (Roasted Pearlspot Fish Curry)

### Ingredients
500 gm pearlspot fish (karimeen)
1/2 cup sambhar onions, peeled
5 flakes garlic
2" piece ginger
6 red chillies
1 tsp pepper
1/4 tsp turmeric powder
2 tomatoes, chopped
2 big onions, sliced
2 tsp curry leaves
4 tsp vinegar
1 tsp salt 1/2 cup coconut oil
1 cup first coconut extract

### For the garnishing
1 tsp coriander leaves, chopped
1 tsp mint leaves, chopped

### Method
1. Grind the garlic, sambhar onions, ginger, red chillies, green chillies and pepper to a fine paste.

2. Mix the ground paste, turmeric powder, vinegar and salt till well combined.

3. Heat half the quantity of oil and saute the chopped tomatoes, sliced onion curry leaves and the ground paste for 2-3 minutes.

4. Now spread banana leaves on a flat frying pan and pour over it the remaining quantity of coconut oil.

5. In the meantime clean the fish and make slits in it with a fork.

6. Apply the sauted masala paste on the fish till it is thoroughly coated and spread the remaining on top of it. Top the fish with the greased banana leaves and cover the pan with a lid. Cook the fish on slow fire with occasional turning till it is tender.

7. Pour over the fish the coconut extract and cook further till the liquid is absorbed. Remove from the fire and transfer the contents to a serving dish.

8. Garnish with the chopped coriander and the mint leaves.

9. Serve hot with rice.

# Kappa Meen Curry
## (Tapioca-n-Fish Curry)

**Ingredients**
2 medium sized tapioca
12 sardines
1 cup freshly grated coconut
2 cups tamarind juice
1 tsp chilli juice
1/4 tsp turmeric powder
3 green chillies, chopped
1" piece ginger, chopped
1 tsp salt

**For the seasoning**
4 tsp coconut oil
2 tsp curry leaves
1/2 tsp mustard seeds

**For the garnishing**

2 tsp grated and roasted coconut
1 tsp coriander leaves
2 tapioca chips, crushed

**Method**

1.  Clean the sardines and keep aside.

2.  Wash, peel and cut the tapioca into cubes.

3.  Pressure cook the tapioca with the half quantity of salt and enough water.

4.  Grind the coconut to a fine paste.

5.  Mix the tamarind juice, chilli powder, turmeric powder, chopped chillies, chopped ginger with the remaining quantity of salt till well combined. Add sardines and bring the contents to boil and cook till the sardines are tender.

6.  Heat oil and saute the seasoning ingredients and the ground paste for a minute.

7.  Add the cooked sardines, cooked tapioca and mix the contents well. Cool for 3-4 minutes. Remove it from fire and transfer the contents to a serving dish.

8.  Garnish it with the roasted coconut, coriander leaves and the crushed tapioca chips.

9.  Serve hot with rice.

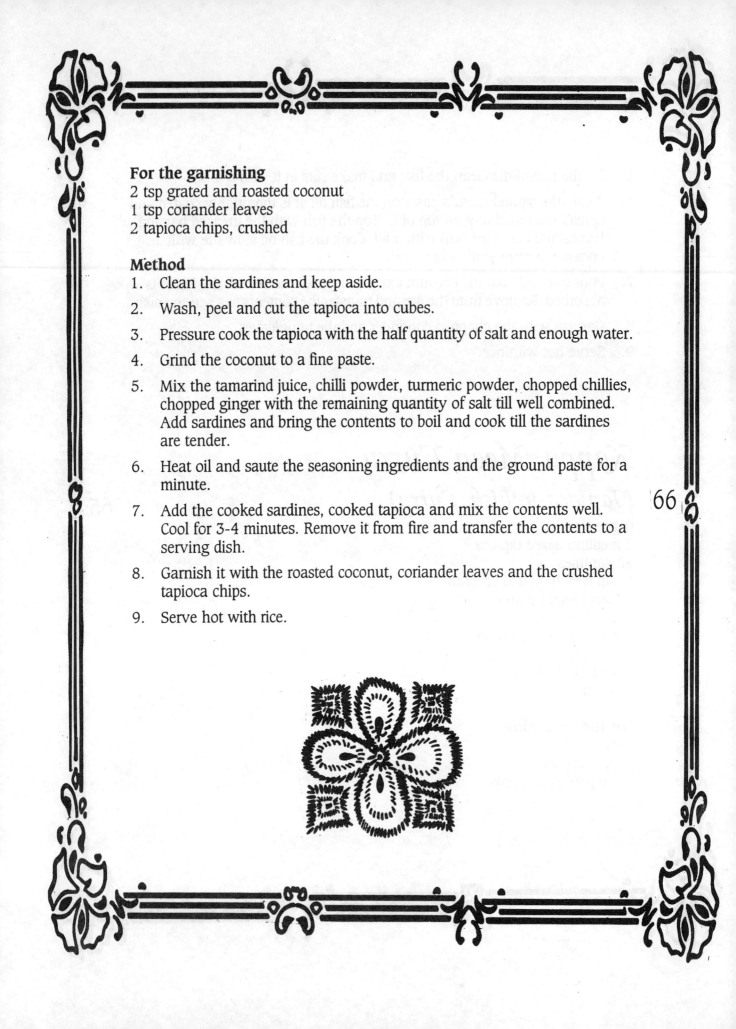

# Koorka Meen Curry

## (Koorka Root Vegetable-n-Fish Curry)

### Ingredients
250 gm koorka root vegetable
12 sardines
1 cup freshly grated coconut
4 onions, peeled
4 flakes garlic
4 green chillies
1" piece ginger
1/2 tsp pepper
1/2 tsp cumin seeds
1/2 tsp fenugreek seeds
1 tsp salt

### For the seasoning
4 tsp coconut oil
2 tsp curry eaves
1/2 tsp mustered seeds
2 red chillies, broken into bits

### For the garnishing
2 tsp coriander leaves, chopped
2 tsp mint leaves chopped

### Method
1. Wash, peel and cook the koorka vegetable with half the quantity of salt and enough water till tender or cook and peel.

2. Clean the sardines and keep aside.

3. Roast the pepper, cumin and the fenugreek seeds and powder together.

67

4. Grind the coconut, onions, garlic, green chillies and ginger to a fine paste with the remaining quantity of salt.

5. Apply the ground paste on the sardines and allow to marinate for 2 hours.

6. Heat oil and saute the seasoning ingredients, for a minute.

7. Add the marinated fish, cover the pan with a lid and cook on slow fire with occasional turning till the fish is tender.

8. Add the cooked koorka vegetable and roasted powder. Mix the contents thoroughly and cook for a minute. Remove from the fire and transfer the contents to a serving dish.

9. Garnish with chopped coriander and mint leaves.

10. Serve hot with rice.

# Vazhakka (Orethakai) - Unnakkammeen Curry
## (Raw Banana-n-dry Fish Curry)

**Ingredients**
2 raw bananas
250 gm dry fish
4 green chillies, slit lengthwise
1/2 cup freshly grated coconut
1 tsp chilli powder
1/2 tsp coriander powder
1/4 tsp turmeric powder
1 tsp salt

**For the seasoning**
4 tsp coconut oil
6 small sambhar onions, peeled and sliced
2 tsp curry leaves

**For the garnishing**
1/2 cup banana chips

**Method**
1.  Wash, peel and cut the bananas into thin strips.

2.  Cut the fish also into thin strips.

3.  Grind coconut to a fine paste.

4.  Mix the banana strips, fish strips, slit green chillies, ground coconut, chilli powder, coriander powder, turmeric powder and salt till well combined. Add to it 1 cup of water and cook till tender on slow fire.

5.  Heat oil and saute the seasoning ingredients. Add the cooked curry and mix well. Cook for a minute. Remove it from slow fire and transfer the contents to a serving dish.

6.  Garnish it with the banana chips.

7.  Serve hot with rice.

# Pollicha Meen Curry

## (Baked Fish Curry)

**Ingredients**
500 gm pomfret
2 tsp ginger-garlic-green chilli paste
1 tsp coriander seeds
1 tsp fennel seeds
1/2 cup freshly grated coconut
1/2 cup small sambhar onions, peeled
1/2 cup vinegar
1 tsp salt
4 tsp coconut oil

**For the garnishing**

2 tsp fresh coconut oil
2 tsp curry leaves, roasted
1 tsp coriander leaves, chopped

**Method**

1. Clean fish and cut it into large pieces. Make slits with a fork.

2. Roast the coriander seeds into the fennel seeds and grind it to a paste.

3. Grind the coconut and the sambhar onions to a paste.

4. Mix the masala, seed and coconut paste and the salt till well combined.

5. Smear the fish pieces with the paste.

6. Grease the banana leaves with the coconut oil and line it on a thick bottomed pan. Place the fish pieces on it. Pour vinegar over the pieces and cover it again with the greased banana leaves. Cover it with the lid and place on the lid red coals. Cook the fish on slow fire till tender. The same dish can be made in an electric oven.

7. Remove the contents from the fire and transfer to a serving dish.

8. Garnish it with roasted curry leaves and the chopped coriander leaves. Spoon coconut oil over it.

9. Serve hot with rice.

# Egg
# &
# Chicken Dishes

71

# Kozhimutta-Urula Kizhanga Curry

## (Egg-n-Potato Curry)

**Ingredients**

4 eggs
4 potatoes
100 gm sambhar onions, peeled and sliced
1/2 cup freshly grated coconut
3 green chillies
1" piece ginger
4 flakes garlic
1/2 tsp garam masala powder
2 tsp vinegar
1 tsp salt
1/4 cup coconut oil

**Garnishing**

2 tsp chopped (mixed) nuts, fried

**Method**

1.  Hard boil the eggs, shell and slice lengthwise into two halves.

2.  Grind the coconut, chillies, ginger and garlic to a fine paste.

3.  Wash, peel and chop the potatoes.

4.  Heat oil and saute the onions for a minute.

5.  Add the ground paste and the chopped potatoes and saute for a minute.

6.  Add garam masala powder, salt with 1 cup of water and cook till the potatoes are tender.

7.  Add the eggs and vinegar. Mix the contents well and cook for 2-3 minutes. Remove it from the fire and transfer the contents to a serving dish.

8.  Garnish it with the chopped and fried nuts.

9.  Serve hot with rice and pappadam.

# Malabar Kozhimutta-Thenga Curry
## (Malabar Egg-n-Coconut Curry)

**Ingredients**

5 eggs
100 gm sambhar onions, peeled and sliced
1 coconut, grated
1/2 cup freshly grated coconut
4 red chillies
1 tsp coriander seeds
1 cup mixed vegetables, chopped
2 tomatoes, chopped
1" ginger, minced
3 green chillies, minced
3 flakes garlic, minced
1 tsp garam masala powder
2 tsp vinegar
1/2 tsp salt

**For the seasoning**

1/4 cup coconut oil
2 tsp curry leaves
1 tsp cumin seeds
1/2 tsp mustard seeds

**For the garnishing**

3 onion and 3 tomato slices

**Method**

1.  Hard boil the eggs, shell and slice lengthwise into two equal halves.

2.  Prepare two extracts with the coconut, first with 1 cup of warm water and the second with 2 cups of warm water.

3.  Roast the grated coconut, red chillies and the coriander seeds and powder.

4.  Heat oil and saute the seasoning ingredients, chopped vegetables, chopped tomatoes, sliced onion, minced ginger, green chillies and the garlic for 2-3 minutes.

5. Add second extract, salt and cook for ten minutes till the vegetables are tender.

6. Add the first extract eggs, garam masala powder, roasted powder and vinegar. Mix the contents well and cook for 2 minutes. Remove it from fire and transfer the contents to a serving dish.

7. Garnish it with the onion and the tomato slices.

8. Serve hot with rice.

# Kerala Kozhimutta Curry

## (Egg Curry Kerala Style)

### Ingredients

5 eggs, beaten thoroughly
1 cup freshly grated coconut
2 tsp ginger-garlic-green chilli paste
1 cup sambhar onions, peeled and sliced
2 tsp curry leaves
1 tsp salt
1/4 cup coconut oil

### For the garnishing

2 tsp fried coconut slices
2 tsp chopped and fried nuts

### Method

1. Mix the beaten eggs, grated coconut, masala paste, sliced onions, curry leaves and salt till well combined.

2. Heat oil in a pan and add the mixture. Stir it when it is set and cook the egg in scramble style. Remove it from the fire and transfer the contents to a serving dish.

3. Garnish the dish with fried coconut slices and the fried nuts.

4. Serve hot with rice and pappadam.

# Kozhierchi Thoran
## (Coconut based Chicken Curry)

### Ingredients

1 chicken, cut into pieces
4 onions, peeled and sliced
1 tsp ginger-garlic paste
4 green chillies, slit lengthwise
1 tsp coriander powder
1 tsp chilli powder
1 cup freshly grated coconut
1 tsp garam masala powder
1 tsp salt
1/4 cup coconut oil

### For the garnishing

2 tsp nuts, grated
2 tsp curry leaves, roasted

76

### Method

1. Heat oil in a pan and saute the onion slices, masala paste, slit chillies, coriander powder, chilli powder for a minute.

2. Add chicken pieces, salt and enough water. Cook till the contents are tender.

3. Add the grated coconut, mix the contents thoroughly and cook for five more minutes. Remove it from the fire and transfer the contents to serving dish.

4. Garnish it with the grated nuts and roasted curry leaves.

5. Serve hot with rice and pappadam.

# Kozhierchi Curry

## (Chicken Curry)

### Ingredients
500 gm chicken
4 onions, sliced
6 flakes garlic, minced
1" ginger, minced
1 coconut, grated
1 tsp chilli powder
1/4 tsp turmeric powder
1 tsp garam masala powder
2 tsp coriander powder
1 tsp pepper powder
1 tsp mustard seeds

### For the seasoning
4 tsp coconut oil
2 tsp curry leaves
1/2 tsp mustard seeds

### For the garnishing
6-8 fried small sambhar onions
2 tsp coriander leaves

### Method
1. Prepare 2 extracts with the coconut, the first with 1 cup of warm water and the second with 2 cups of warm water.

2. Heat oil and saute the seasoning ingredients, sliced onions and minced ginger garlic for a minute.

3. Add the chicken pieces, salt, chilli powder, turmeric powder and second coconut extract. Cook 'ill the chicken is tender.

77

4. Add the first coconut extract, garam masala powder, coriander and the pepper powder and cook for five minutes. Remove from the fire and transfer the contents to a serving dish.

5. Garnish it with the fried sambhar onions and the coriander leaves.

6. Serve hot with rice.

# Kozhierchi Varthada

## (Chicken Roast)

**Ingredients**
1 chicken
1/2 coconut, grated
2 tsp chilli powder
2 tsp coriander powder
2 tsp garam masala powder
3 tsp pepper powder
1/4 tsp turmeric powder
100 gm sambhar onions, peeled
5 flakes garlic
1 tsp cumin seeds
4 tsp coconut oil
4 tsp vinegar
1 tsp salt

**For the garnishing**
1 tsp curry leaves,
roasted banana chips and tapioca chips

**Method**

1. Grind the coconut, onions, green chillies, ginger, garlic and the cumin seeds to a fine paste.

2. Mix the ground paste with the chilli powder, coriander powder, garam masala powder, pepper powder, turmeric powder, coconut oil, vinegar and the salt till well combined.

3. In the meantime, wash, clean the chicken and scoop out the insides.

4. Slit the chicken on all sides with a fork.

5. Stuff the chicken with the prepared mixture and also coat it on the outside.

6. Leave the chicken aside for 2 hours, to marinate.

7. Roast the chicken on hot coals or grill it on a gas stove or bake it in a greased oven dish till tender and juicy.

8. Transfer the chicken to a serving dish.

9. Garnish it with the roasted curry leaves and the chips.

10. Serve hot with rice.

79

# Kozhierchi Porichadhu

## (Fried Chicken)

**Ingredients**
500 gm chicken pieces
1/4 kg sambhar onions, peeled
3 red chillies
3 green chillies
4 flakes garlic
1" piece ginger
1/4 tsp turmeric powder
1 tsp garam masala powder
4 tsp vinegar
1 tsp salt
1/2 cup coconut oil

**For the garnishing**

3 onions slices

3 tomato slices

1 tsp chopped coriander leaves

**Method**

1. Grind the sambhar onions, red chillies, green chillies, garlic and ginger to a fine paste.

2. Mix the ground paste with the turmeric powder, garam masala powder, vinegar and salt till well combined.

3. Apply the paste to the chicken pieces and allow it to marinate for 2 hours.

4. Heat oil and fry the chicken pieces till tender and golden. Drain well and transfer the contents to a serving dish.

5. Garnish it with onion slices, tomato slices and the chopped coriander leaves.

6. Serve hot with rice.

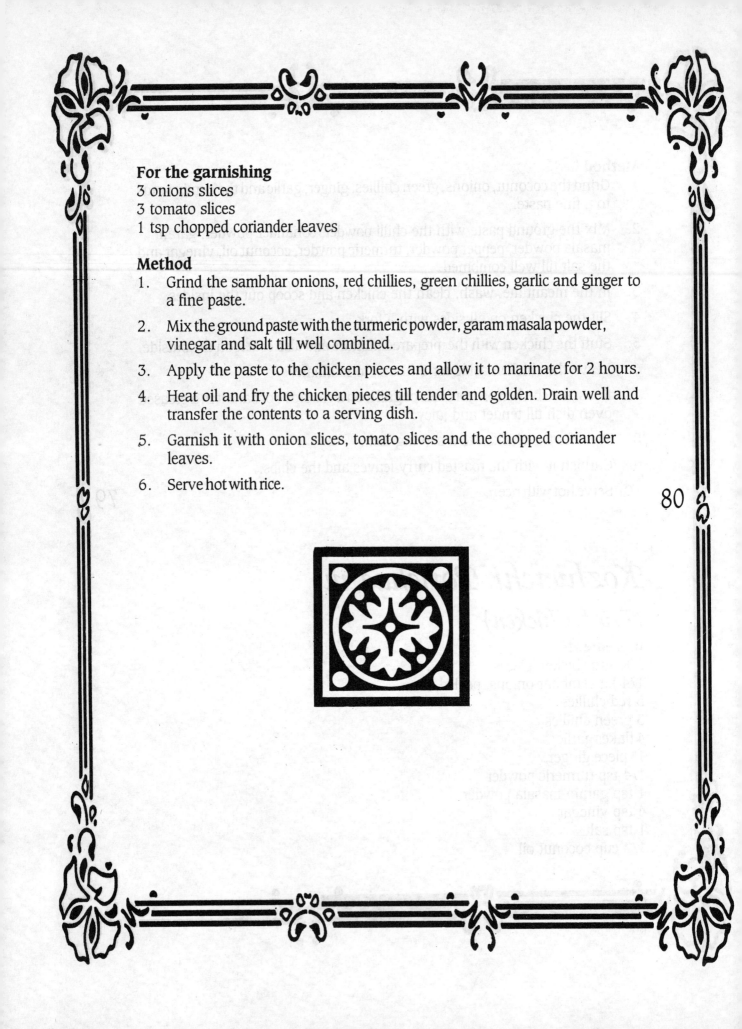

# *Mutton Dishes*

81

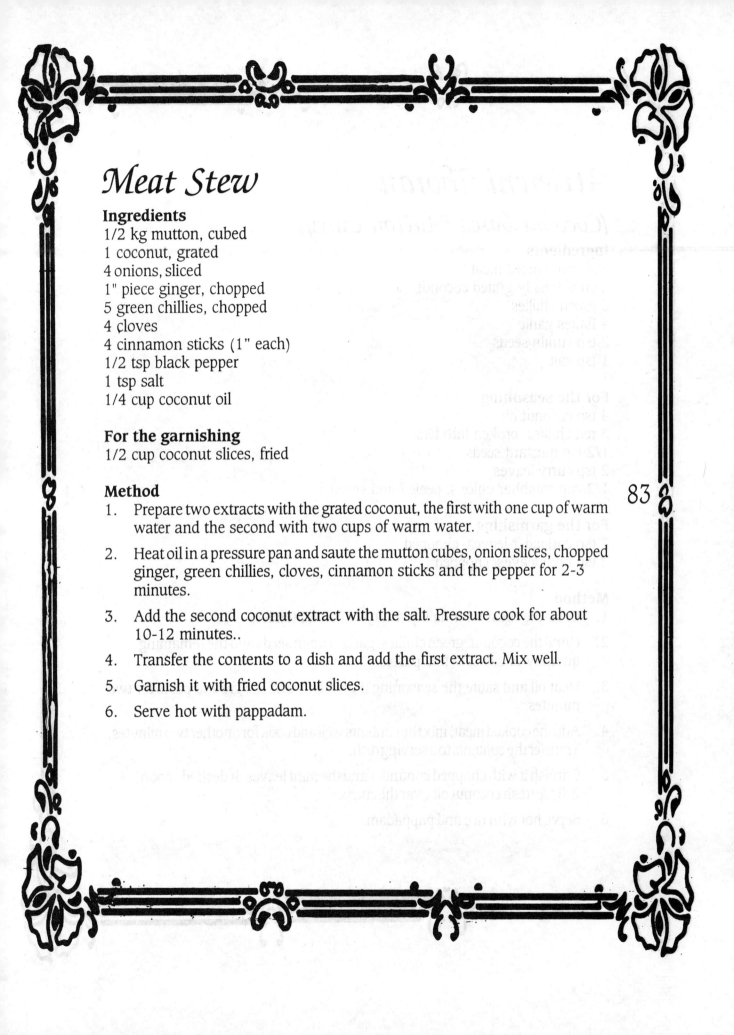

# Meat Stew

### Ingredients
1/2 kg mutton, cubed
1 coconut, grated
4 onions, sliced
1" piece ginger, chopped
5 green chillies, chopped
4 cloves
4 cinnamon sticks (1" each)
1/2 tsp black pepper
1 tsp salt
1/4 cup coconut oil

### For the garnishing
1/2 cup coconut slices, fried

### Method
1. Prepare two extracts with the grated coconut, the first with one cup of warm water and the second with two cups of warm water.

2. Heat oil in a pressure pan and saute the mutton cubes, onion slices, chopped ginger, green chillies, cloves, cinnamon sticks and the pepper for 2-3 minutes.

3. Add the second coconut extract with the salt. Pressure cook for about 10-12 minutes..

4. Transfer the contents to a dish and add the first extract. Mix well.

5. Garnish it with fried coconut slices.

6. Serve hot with pappadam.

83

# Attierchi Thoran

## (Coconut based Mutton Curry)

### Ingredients
500 gm minced meat
2 cups freshly grated coconut
5 green chillies
4 flakes garlic
2 tsp cumin seeds
1 tsp salt

### For the seasoning
4 tsp coconut oil
3 red chillies, broken into bits
1/2 tsp mustard seeds
2 tsp curry leaves
1/2 cup sambhar onions, peeled and sliced

### For the garnishing
2 tsp coriander leaves, chopped
2 tsp mint leaves, chopped

### Method
1. Cook the meat with half quantity of salt till tender.

2. Grind the coconut, green chillies, garlic, cumin seeds and the remaining quantity of salt to a fine paste.

3. Heat oil and saute the seasoning ingredients and the ground paste for two minutes.

4. Add the cooked meat, mix the contents well and cook for another two minutes. Transfer the contents to a serving dish.

5. Garnish it with chopped coriander and the mint leaves. If desired spoon 2-3 tsp fresh coconut oil over the curry.

6. Serve hot with rice and pappadam.

# Malabar Attierchi Curry
## (Malabar Mutton Curry)

**Ingredients**

1/2 kg mutton, cubed
1 cup first extract of coconut milk
6 onions, sliced
2 tsp curry leaves
1 tsp coriander seeds
1 tsp cumin seeds
3 red chillies
1/2 tsp pepper
6 cloves
1 tsp garam masala powder
5 flakes garlic
5 green chillies
1" ginger
1 tsp salt
1/2 cup coconut oil

**For the garnishing**

2 tsp grated and roasted coconut

**Method**

1. Roast the coriander seeds, curry leaves, cumin seeds, red chillies, pepper and cloves. Powder all together.

2. Grind ginger, garlic and the green chillies to a fine paste.

3. Heat oil and saute the sliced onion and the mutton cubes for 2-3 minutes.

4. Add 2 cups of water and cook for 10 minutes.

5. Add salt, garam masala powder, ground paste, roasted powder and the coconut milk. Mix the contents well and cook for 5 minutes. Remove it from the fire and transfer the contents to a serving dish.

6. Garnish it with grated and the roasted coconut.

7. Serve hot with rice.

# Attierchi Porichadhu
## (Mutton Fry)

### Ingredients
500 gm mutton cubes
1/4 kg sambhar onions, peeled
3 red chillies
3 green chillies
5 flakes garlic
1" piece ginger
1 tsp garam masala powder
1/4 tsp turmeric powder
1 tsp salt
1/2 cup coconut oil

### For the garnishing
2 onion slices, 2 tomato slices and 2 cucumber slices

86

### Method
1. Grind the onions, green chillies, red chillies, garlic and ginger to a fine paste.

2. Mix the ground paste with the garam masala powder, turmeric powder vinegar and salt till well combined.

3. Apply the marinade to the mutton cubes and allow it to marinate for two hours.

4. Heat oil and fry the mutton pieces till crisp and brown. Drain well.

5. Transfer the contents to a serving dish.

6. Garnish it with onion, tomato and the cucumber slices.

7. Serve hot with rice.

# Attierchi-Urla Kizhanga Curry

## (Mutton-n-Potato Curry)

**Ingredients**
250 gm mutton cubes
4 potatoes
4 green chillies, slit lengthwise
1" piece ginger, cut into thin strips
5 flakes garlic, cut into thin strips
1 coconut, grated
1 tsp coriander powder
1 tsp pepper powder
1 tsp garam masala powder
1 tsp vinegar
1 tsp salt
1/4 tsp chilli powder
1/4 tsp turmeric powder

**For the seasoning**
4 tsp coconut oil
1/2 cup sambhar onions, peeled and sliced
1/2 tsp mustard seeds

**For the garnishing**
2 tsp roasted curry leaves
2 tsp chopped mint leaves

**Method**
1. Pressure cook mutton cubes with half the quantity of salt.

2. Wash, peel and cut the potatoes into cubes. Cook with the remaining quantity of salt till tender.

3. Prepare two extracts with coconut each with 1 cup of warm water.

4.  Heat oil and saute the seasoning ingredients, green chillies, ginger and the garlic. Add second extract, cooked mutton and the potato, coriander powder, pepper powder, garam masala powder, vinegar, chilli and the turmeric powder. Mix well and cook for five minutes till dry.

5.  Add first extract, cook for a minute and remove it from fire. Transfer the contents to a serving dish.

6.  Garnish it with roasted curry leaves and the chopped mint leaves.

# Malabar Meat Ball Curry

## Ingredients

### For the meat balls
350 gm meat, minced
4 onions
2" piece ginger
4 green chillies
1/2 tsp salt

### For the curry
1 coconut, grated
5 flakes garlic
1" piece ginger
4 red chillies
2 tsp coriander seeds
1 tsp sesame seeds
1 tsp garam masala powder
1 tsp pepper powder
1 tsp cumin seed powder
1/4 cup vinegar
1/2 tsp salt

**For the seasoning**
4 tsp coconut oil
2 tsp curry leaves
6 sambhar onions, peeled and sliced
1/2 tsp mustard seeds

**For the garnishing**
2 tsp chopped coriander leaves and 2 tsp chopped onion

**Method**
1. Grind onions, green chillies and the ginger to a fine paste.

2. Mix the minced meat, ground paste and the salt till well combined.

3. Shape the contents into round balls.

4. Prepare two extracts with the grated coconut, first with 1 cup of warm water and second with 2 cups of warm water.

5. Grind garlic, ginger and the greeen chillies to a fine paste.

6. Roast the red chillies, coriander seeds and the sesame seeds and powder.

7. Heat oil and saute the seasoning ingredients and the ground paste.

8. Add the second coconut extract, roasted powder, garam masala powder, pepper powder, cumin powder, vinegar and salt. Mix the contents thoroughly.

9. Place the meat balls carefully in the gravy, cover it with a lid and cook on slow fire till the meat balls are tender.

10. Add the first coconut extract and cook for five minutes. Mix well and cook for five more minutes.

11. Remove from the fire and transfer the contents to a serving dish.

12. Garnish with chopped coriander leaves and chopped onion.

13. Serve hot with rice.

89

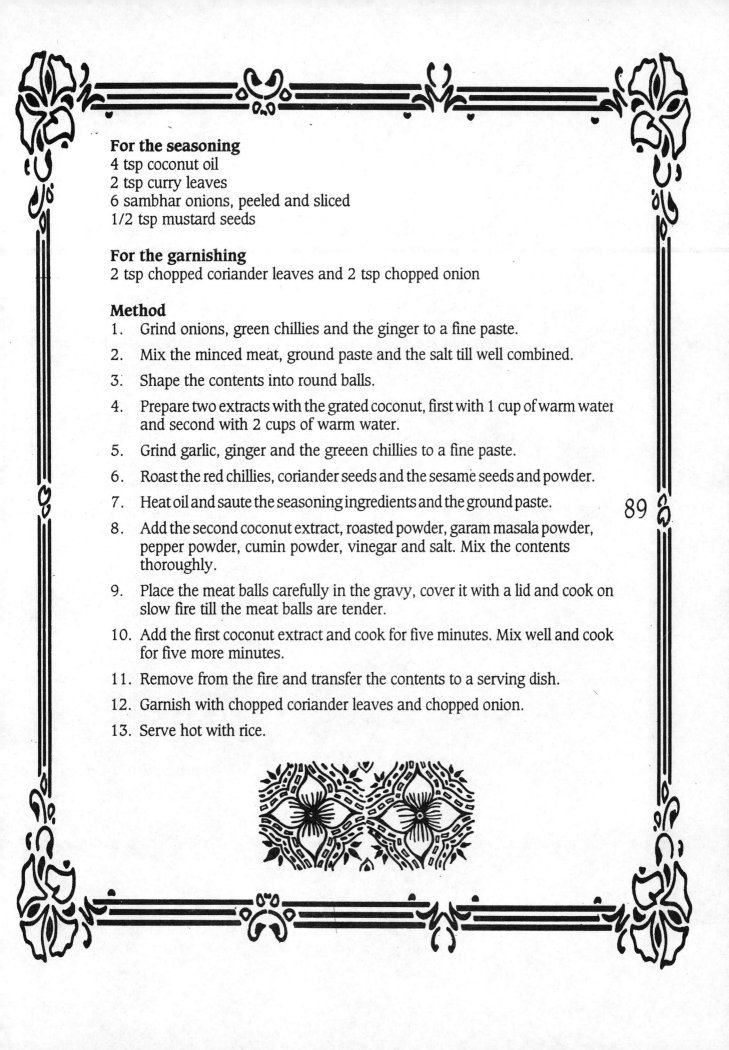

# Pork Dishes

Pork Dishes

# Pannierchi Curry

## (Pork Curry)

**Ingredinets**

500 gm pork
5 green chillies
2" piece ginger
5 flakes garlic
3 tomatoes, chopped
3 onions, sliced
1 tsp coriander powder
2 tsp garam masala powder
1 cup coconut milk (first extract)
1 tsp salt
1/4 cup coconut coil

**For the seasoning**

1/2 tsp mustard and 1/2 tsp cumin seeds

**For the garnishing**

2 tsp grated and roasted coconut
2 tsp curry leaves, roasted or fried.

**Method**

1.  Cut the pork into small pieces

2.  Pressure cook the pork with salt and enough water.

3.  Grind green chillies, garlic and the ginger to a fine paste.

4.  Heat oil and saute seasoning ingredients, ground paste, chopped tomatoes and the onion slices for 2-3 minutes.

5.  Add the cooked pork, coconut milk, coriander powder, garam masala powder and mix the contents well. Cook for 5 more mintues and remove it from fire. Transfer the contents to a serving dish.

6.  Garnish it with the roasted coconut and the curry leaves.

7.  Serve hot with rice.

# Pannierchi Vazhathiyadhu

## (Sauted Pork Curry)

### Ingredients
500 gm pork
5 green chillies, chopped
1" piece ginger, chopped
5 flakes garlic, chopped
3 onions, chopped
1 tsp chilli powder
1 tsp pepper powder
1 tsp garam masala powder
1 tsp salt
1/4 tsp turmeric powder
1/4 cup coconut oil

### For the garnishing
2 tsp grated cheese

94

### Method

1.  Cut the pork into medium size piece .

2.  Mix the coriander powder, chilli powder, pepper powder, garam masala powder and salt till well combined.

3.  Mix the pork with the required amount of water and pressure cook.

4.  Heat oil and saute the chopped ingredients and the cooked pork on slow fire for 20 minutes. Remove from the fire and transfer the contents to a serving dish.

5.  Garnish the sauted pork curry with the grated cheese.

6.  Serve hot with rice and pappadam.

# Pannierchi Porichadhu

## (Pork Fry)

### Ingredients

500 gm pork, cut into big pieces
2 tsp chilli powder
1 tsp pepper powder
1/4 tsp turmeric powder
2 tsp garam masala powder
1/4 cup vinegar
2 tsp salt
coconut oil for frying

### For the garnishing

2 onion, 2 tomato and 2 cucumber slices

### Method

1. Mix chilli powder, pepper powder, turmeric powder, garam masala powder, vinegar and salt till well combined.

2. Apply the mixture to the pork pieces and allow it to marinate for 2 hours.

3. Fry in oil till golden. Drain well.

4. Transfer the contents to the serving dish.

5. Garnish it with onion, tomato and the cucumber slices.

6. Serve hot with rice.

# Snacks

# Upperi (Chips)

# Vazhakka Upperi

## (Banana Chips)

**Ingredients**

6 malabar raw plantains
Salt to taste
Coconut oil for frying

**Method**

1. Wash, peel and slice the bananas as thin as possible.

2. Heat oil and fry the slices. When half done, reduce heat and sprinkle salt solution over the chips.

3. Increase heat and fry the chips till crisp. Drain well.

4. If desired sprinkle chilli powder on chips.

5. Serve as a snack or as a side dish with lunch or dinner along with rice.

In the case of jackfruit, the hard portion should be removed and the soft portion should be sliced as thin as possible. Repeat the same method as mentioned for the banana chips.

To prepare the tapioca chips, wash, peel and slice the root vegetable as thin as possible. Then repeat the same method mentioned above for the banana chips.

The chips can be preserved for over a month in sterile jars and tins.

# Puttu

## *(Rice-n-Coconut Delicacy)*

**Ingredients**

2 cups rice flour
2 cups freshly grated coconut
1 tsp salt
For the topping
3 tsp ghee or coconut oil

**Method**

1. Roast the rice flour till the raw smell disappears. Allow it to cool.

2. Mix the roasted rice and the salt well.

3. Sprinkle little quantity of water on the rice flour till moist.

4. Sprinkle little grated coconut at the bottom of the putu vessel.

5. Spread little moist flour on it, followed by the grated coconut.

6. Continue layering till the cylinder is filled, finishing with a coconut layer

7. Cover the puttu vessel with a lid and steam for 10 minutes.

8. Remove the lid and push the puttu with the help of a round rod, onto a serving plate.

9. Slice the puttu into two inch pieces.

10. Spoon ghee or coconut oil over it.

11. Serve with chutney or any gravy curry for breakfast.

100

# Chakka Pazham Puttu
## (Jackfruit-n-Coconut Delight)

**Ingredients**

2 cups rice flour
1 cup ripe jackfruit, chopped
1 cup freshly grated coconut
A pinch of salt

**For the topping**

3 tsp ghee or coconut oil

**Method**

1. Roast the rice flour till the raw smell disappears. Allow it to cool.

2. Mix the roasted rice flour, chopped jackfruit, half the quantity of grated coconut and a pinch of salt till well combined.

3. Sprinkle little quantity of water on the above mixture till it is moist. Mix well.

4. Sprinkle little grated coconut at the bottom of the puttu vessel.

5. Spread little moist flour on it, followed by the grated coconut.

6. Continue layering till the cylinder is filled, finishing with a coconut layer.

7. Cover the puttu vessel with a lid and steam it for about ten minutes.

8. Remove the lid and push the puttu with the help of a round rod onto a serving plate.

9. Slice the puttu into two inch pieces.

10. Spoon ghee over the puttu and serve hot with chutney or any gravy curry for breakfast.

# Manga Pazham Putu
## (Mango-n-Coconut Delicacy)

### Ingredients
2 cups rice flour
1 cup mango, chopped
1 cup freshly grated coconut
A pinch of salt

### For the topping
3 tsp ghee or melted butter or coconut oil
1 tsp cardamom powder

### Method
1. Roast the rice flour till the raw smell disappears. Allow it to cool.

2. Mix the rice flour, chopped mango, half the quantity of grated coconut and a pinch of salt.

3. Sprinkle some grated coconut at the bottom of the puttu vessel.

4. Top it with little quantity of mango mixture followed by grated coconut. Continue layering and end it with the grated coconut.

5. Cover the puttu vessel with the lid and steam it for about ten minutes.

6. Remove the lid and push the puttu with a round rod, on to a serving plate.

7. Slice the puttu into two inch pieces.

8. Spoon ghee or coconut oil over the slices.

9. Sprinkle cardamom powder over the slices.

10. Serve for breakfast with any gravy curry

102

# Vellappam
## (Rice Pancake)

**Ingredients**

4 cups rice, washed and soaked
2 cups freshly grated coconut
1/4 cup powdered sugar
1 tsp cumin seeds
1/2 tsp dry yeast granules
1/2 tsp baking powder
1/2  tsp salt
1/2 cup coconut oil

**For the garnishing**

2 cups roasted curry leaves
2 cups coriander leaves, chopped

103

**Method**

1. Drain the soaked rice and grind it with grated coconut, sugar, cumin seeds and salt with enough quantity of water so as to form a loose batter.

2. Boil 1 cup of the batter and add it to the remaining quantity of batter. Mix the contents well.

3. Dissolve yeast granules in 1/2 cup of warm water and add it to the batter along with the baking powder. Mix the contents thoroughly till well combined.

4. Cover and keep the batter overnight.

5. Pour a spoonfull of batter on a hot tava and spread it slightly. Pour 1 tsp of coconut oil over its edges and cover the pancake with a lid. When the base is golden, turn and cook the other side. Repeat the same till the batter is over.

6. Garnish the pancakes with the roasted curry leaves and the chopped coriander leaves.

7. Serve hot vellappams with gravy mutton curry or gravy potato curry for breakfast.

# Vataiappam
## (Steamed Rice Delicacy)

**Ingredients**

2 cups vellappam batter

**For the garnishing**

3 tsp ghee or coconut oil
1/2 cup cashewnuts, chopped and fried in ghee

**Method**

1. Pour the batter of 2.5 cm thickness onto a greased plate or a container.

2. Steam it for ten minutes.

3. Cut it into required shapes and sizes.

4. Spoon coconut oil or ghee over the pieces and garnish it with fried cashewnuts.

5. Serve with any gravy curry for breakfast.

# Idiappam
## (String Hoppers)

**Ingredients**

4 cups rice flour
1 cup freshgly grated coconut
1/2 cup powdered sugar
1 tsp cardamom powder
1/2 tsp salt

**For the garnishing**

1/2 cup mixed nuts, grated

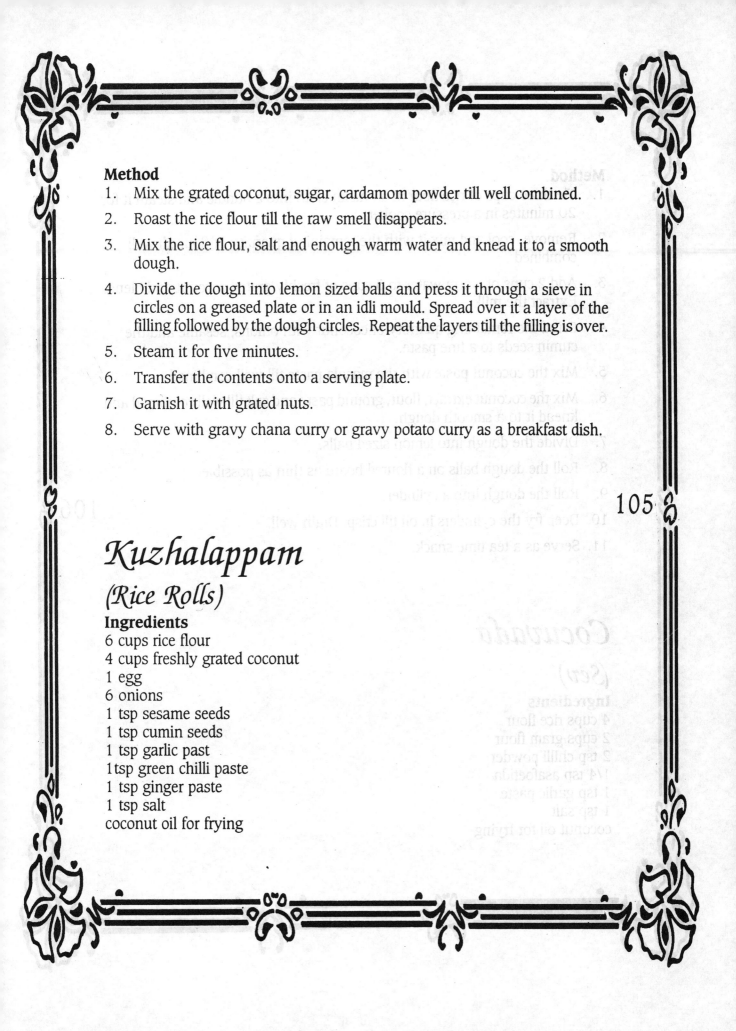

## Method

1. Mix the grated coconut, sugar, cardamom powder till well combined.

2. Roast the rice flour till the raw smell disappears.

3. Mix the rice flour, salt and enough warm water and knead it to a smooth dough.

4. Divide the dough into lemon sized balls and press it through a sieve in circles on a greased plate or in an idli mould. Spread over it a layer of the filling followed by the dough circles. Repeat the layers till the filling is over.

5. Steam it for five minutes.

6. Transfer the contents onto a serving plate.

7. Garnish it with grated nuts.

8. Serve with gravy chana curry or gravy potato curry as a breakfast dish.

# Kuzhalappam

## (Rice Rolls)

### Ingredients
6 cups rice flour
4 cups freshly grated coconut
1 egg
6 onions
1 tsp sesame seeds
1 tsp cumin seeds
1 tsp garlic past
1tsp green chilli paste
1 tsp ginger paste
1 tsp salt
coconut oil for frying

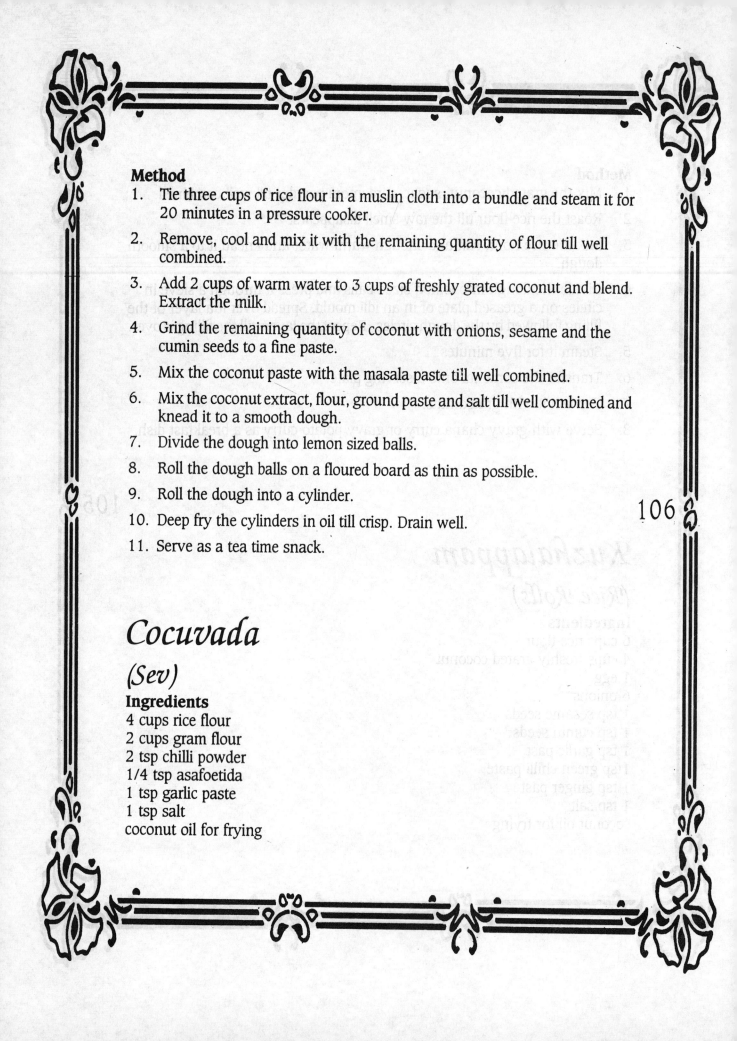

## Method

1. Tie three cups of rice flour in a muslin cloth into a bundle and steam it for 20 minutes in a pressure cooker.

2. Remove, cool and mix it with the remaining quantity of flour till well combined.

3. Add 2 cups of warm water to 3 cups of freshly grated coconut and blend. Extract the milk.

4. Grind the remaining quantity of coconut with onions, sesame and the cumin seeds to a fine paste.

5. Mix the coconut paste with the masala paste till well combined.

6. Mix the coconut extract, flour, ground paste and salt till well combined and knead it to a smooth dough.

7. Divide the dough into lemon sized balls.

8. Roll the dough balls on a floured board as thin as possible.

9. Roll the dough into a cylinder.

10. Deep fry the cylinders in oil till crisp. Drain well.

11. Serve as a tea time snack.

# *Cocuvada*

## *(Sev)*

### Ingredients
4 cups rice flour
2 cups gram flour
2 tsp chilli powder
1/4 tsp asafoetida
1 tsp garlic paste
1 tsp salt
coconut oil for frying

**For the garnishing**
1/2 cup coriander leaves, chopped
1/2 cup onion, chopped

**Method**

1. Mix all the ingredients till well combined.

2. Add water and knead to a smooth dough.

3. Pass the dough through the sieve into hot oil in circles and fry till crisp. Drain well.

4. Garnish the sev with the chopped coriander leaves and the chopped onion.

5. Serve as a teatime snack.

# Pathri

## (Rice Roti)

**Ingredients**
4 cups rice flour
1 tsp salt

**For the topping**
1 cup first coconut extract
Coconut oil or ghee for smearing

**Method**

1. Roast the rice flour till the raw smell disappears.

2. Dissolve salt in the required quantity of warm water and add this gradually to the flour. Knead it to a smooth dough.

3. Divide the dough into lemon size balls.

4. Roll the dough balls on the floured board as thin as possible.

5. Toast it on a tava with coconut oil or ghee till cooked on either side.

6. Serve with coconut extract spooned over the roti or serve smeared with ghee with any gravy curry at any meal time.

# Neyyichoru
## (Ghee Rice)

**Ingredients**

2 cups basmati rice
1/2 cup ghee
4 onions, peeled and sliced
5 cloves
5 cinnamon sticks
3 black cardamoms
5 bay leaves

**For the garnishing**

6-8 cashewnuts, chopped and fried in ghee

**Method**

1. Clean, wash and soak the rice for 20 minutes.

2. Heat ghee and saute the onion and the spices for a minute.

3. Add rice and saute further for a minute.

4. Add 3 cups of water, salt, mix and cook till the rice is tender and dry. Remove from the fire and transfer the contents to a serving dish.

5. Garnish it with roasted cashewnuts.

6. Serve hot with chicken, mutton or any vegetable curry.

# Pappadams
## ( Papad)

### Ingredients
250 gm urad dal or rice
1 tsp pepper powder
1/2 tsp asafoetida
1 tsp salt

### Method
1. Soak the dal overnight. Drain and dry in the sun.

2. Grind the dal to a fine powder.

3. Mix the ground flour, pepper powder, asafoetida and salt till well combined.

4. Add required amount of water gradually to the flour and knead it to a stiff dough.

5. Divide the dough into lemon size balls.

6. Roll them on the floured board as thin as possible.

7. Dry them in the sun for two days and store in air tight jars or tins.

8. Fry in oil when required.

9. Pappadams are best served with lunch or dinner.

109

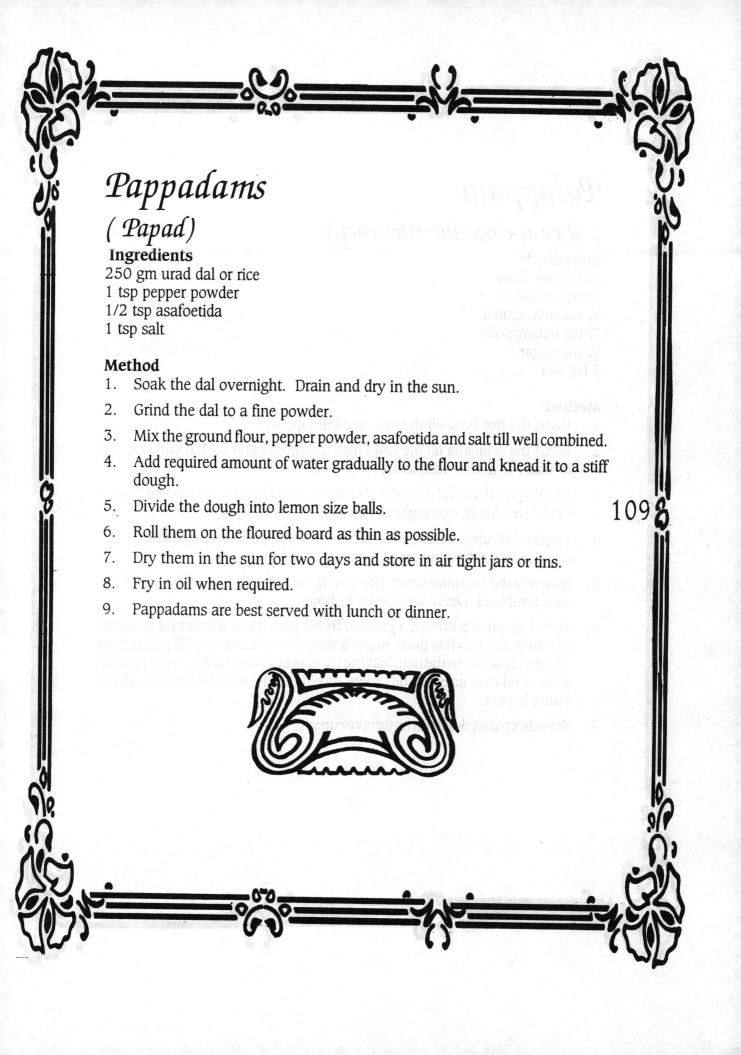

# Palappam

## ( Rice-n-Coconut Delicacy)

### Ingredients

2 cups rice flour
½ cup semolina
½ coconut, grated
½ tsp baking soda
½ cup sugar
1 tsp salt

### Method

1. Roast the rice flour till the raw smell desappears.

2. Roast the semolina till the raw smell disappears and cook it with 1 ½ cup of water to a semi solid state.

3. Mix the rice flour and the cooked semolina and knead it to a smooth dough. Leave the dough overnight to ferment.

4. Prepare 2 ½ cup coconut milk extract from the grated coconut by adding same quantity of warm water.

5. Now mix the coconut extract, rice dough, baking soda, sugar and salt till well combined. Leave it aside for ½ hour.

6. Pour 1 tbspn of batter on a greased frying pan, allow it to set for a minute and twist the pan few times in clock wise or anti-clockwise till a thin layer of batter spreads on the pan, leaving the central portion thick. Toast pouring ghee or oil over its edges till brown on either side. Repeat the same till the batter is over.

7. Serve hot palappams with any gravy curry.

110

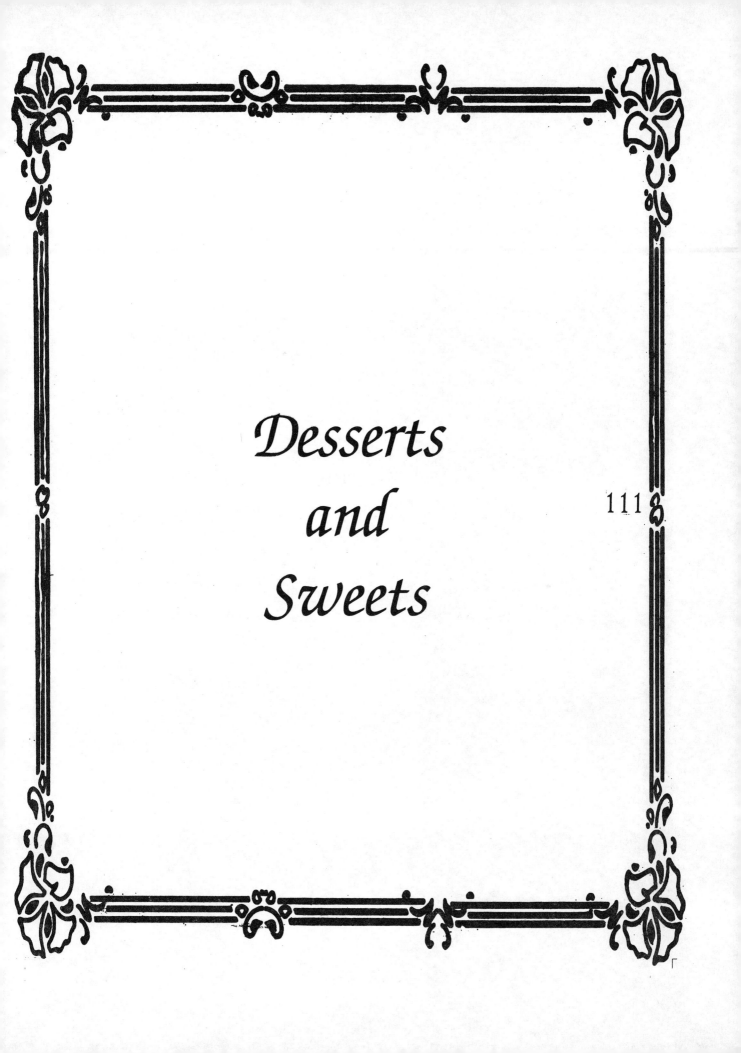

# Desserts
# and
# Sweets

111

# Paalada Pradhaman
## (Rice-n-Milk Pudding)

**Ingredients**
2 litres milk
1 cup rice
1 cup sugar
2 tsp mixed nuts, chopped
1/2 tsp cardamom powder
1/2 tsp saffron strands
1 tsp ghee

**For the garnishing**
2 tsp raisins

**Method**

1. Wash and soak the rice for 30 minutes. Drain well.
2. Grind the rice with half cup of water to a smooth paste.
3. Spread the rice paste on the plantain leaf as thin as possible.
4. Gently roll the leaf and steam for 5 minutes.
5. Shred the cooked rice layer.
6. Boil milk and add sugar, cardamom powder and the saffron strands. Continue to boil till the quantity is slightly reduced.
7. In the meantime, fry the chopped nuts in half the quantity of ghee and add to the pudding.
8. Add the shredded rice and continue to boil for two more minutes.
9. Remove from the fire and transfer the contents to a serving dish.
10. Fry the raisins in the remaining quantity of ghee. Garnish the pudding with the fried raisins.
11. Serve hot or cold as desired.

# Ada Pradhaman
## (Rice-n-Coconut Milk Pudding)

### Ingredients
1/2 cup ada
1 coconut, grated
1 cup jaggery, crumbled
1 tsp cardamom powder
1/4 tsp cumin powder
1/4 tsp dry ginger powder
2 tps mixed nuts, chopped
2 tsp raisins
1 tsp ghee

### For the garnishing
1/2 tsp saffron strands, soaked in 2 tsp hot water

114

### Method
1. Prepare three extracts with the coconut, first with 1 cup of warm water, and second and third with 2 cups of warm water.

2. Boil ada in 2 cups of water till tender and drain well.

3. Dissolve jaggery in the third coconut extract and bring it to a boil.

4. Add ada and cook for 5 minutes.

5. Add second extract and cook for 5 minutes.

6. In the meantime fry the chopped nuts and the raisins in ghee.

7. Add fried nuts, raisins, cardamom powder, cumin powder, dry ginger powder, mix well and cook for a minute.

8. Just before removing the pradhaman from the fire, add the first extract and mix the contents well.

9. Garnish it with the saffron strands.

10. Serve hot or cold as desired.

# Vazhakka Pazham Pradhaman
## (Ripe Malabar Plantain-n-Coconut Milk Pudding,

**Ingredients**

4 ripe Malabar plantains, peeled and sliced
1 coconut, grated
1/2 kg jaggery
1 tsp cardamom powder
4 tsp ghee

**For the garnishing**

1/2 tsp cumin seeds
2 tsp coconut slices

**Method**

1. Prepare two extracts with the coconut, first with 1 cup of warm water and the second with 3 cups of warm water.

2. Boil the banana slices in the second extract for 5 minutes.

3. Add the grated jaggery and 2 tsp ghee and cook till the syrup thickens.

4. Add the cardamom powder and cook for a minute.

5. Add the first extract, mix the contents well and remove it from fire. Transfer the contents to a serving dish.

6. Heat the remaining quantity of ghee and saute the cumin seeds and the coconut slices. Garnish the pudding with it.

7. Serve hot or cold as desired.

# Manga Pazham Pradhaman
## (Ripe Mango-n-Coconut Milk Pudding)

**Ingredients**

1 coconut, grated
1 cup mango pulp
1 cup jaggery, crumbled
1 tsp milk masala powder
2 tsp raisins
1 tsp ghee
1/4 tsp cumin powder
1/4 tsp dry ginger powder

**For the garnishing**
2 tsp mixed nuts, chopped, and fried ghee

**Method**

1. Prepare two extracts with the coconut, first with 1 cup of warm water and the second with 3 cups of warm water.

2. Dissolve jaggery in the second extract and bring it to a boil.

3. Add the mango pulp, and cook till it thickens.

4. Add the milk masala powder, cumin powder, dry ginger powder and cook for a minute.

5. Heat ghee and fry the raisins.

6. Add the raisins, first extract, mix the contents well and remove from the fire. Transfer the contents to a serving dish.

7. Garnish it with the fried nuts.

8. Serve hot or cold as desired.

# Chakka Pazham Pradhaman
## (Jackfruit-n-Coconut Milk Pudding)

### Ingredients
1 coconut, grated
1 cup ripe jackfruit pulps
1 cup jaggery, crumbled
`1 tsp cardamom powder
1/4 tsp cumin powder1/2 tsp safforn strands, soaked in 2 tsp hot water

### For the garnishing
2 tsp chopped nuts, fried in ghee

### Method
1. Prepare two extracts with the coconut, first with 1 cup of warm water and the second with 3 cups of warm water.

2. Dissolve the jaggery in the second extract and bring the contents to boil for 5 minutes.

3. Add the jackfruit pulp, mix well and cook till it thickens.

4. Add the cardamom powder, cumin powder and the saffron water, mix well and cook for a minute.

5. Add the first extract, mix well and remove from the fire. Transfer the contents to a serving dish.

6. Garnish it with the fried nuts.

7. Serve hot or cold as desired.

117

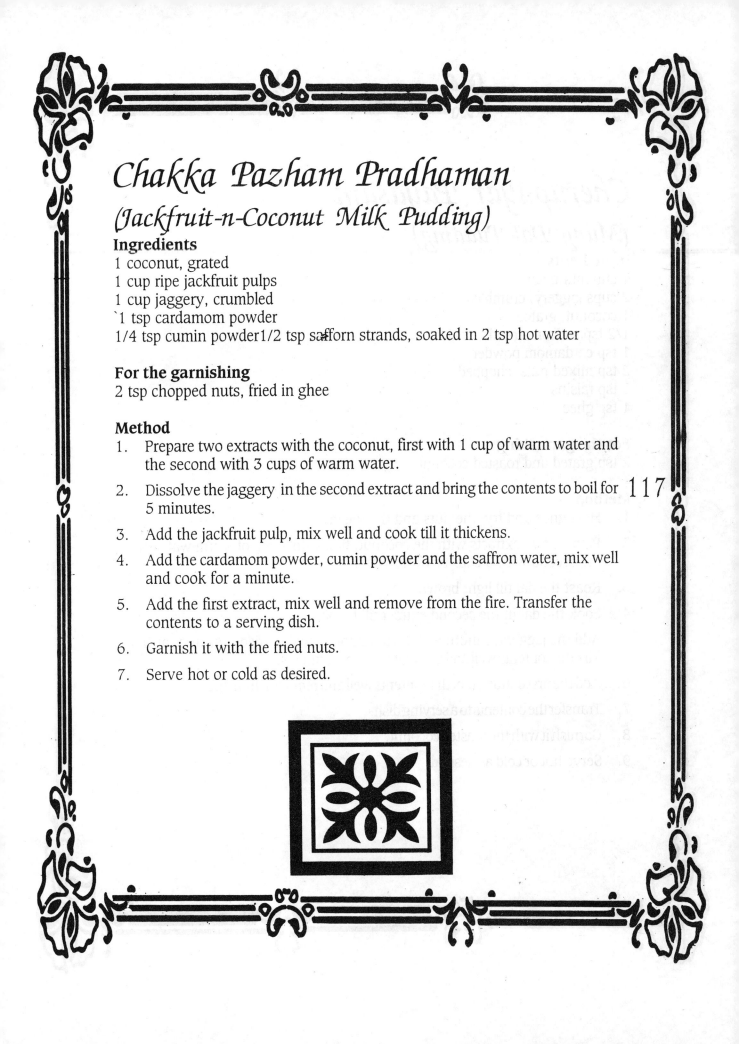

# Cherupayar Payasam
## (Mung Dal Pudding)

### Ingredients
1 cup mung dal
2 cups jaggery, crumbled
1 coconut, grated
1/2 tsp saffron strands, soaked in 2 tsp hot water
1 tsp cardamom powder
2 tsp mixed nuts, chopped
2 tsp raisins
1 tsp ghee

### For the garnishing
2 tsp grated and roasted coconut

### Method
1. Heat ghee and fry the nuts and the raisins.

2. Prepare two extracts with the coconut, first with 1 cup of warm water and the second with 3 cups of warm water.

3. Roast the dal till light brown.

4. Cook the dal in the second extract till tender.

5. Add the jaggery, safforn water, cardamom powder, fried nuts and raisins, Mix the contents well and cook for five more minutes.

6. Add the first extract, mix the contents well and remove it from fire.

7. Transfer the contents to a serving dish.

8. Garnish it with the roasted coconut.

9. Serve hot or cold as desired.

118

# Chakka Pazham Halwa

## (Ripe Jackfruit Halwa)

**Ingredients**

500 gm ripe jackfruit, minced
500 gm jaggery, crumbled
1/2 cup ghee
1 tsp  cardamom powder
2 tsp mixed nuts, chopped
2 tsp raisins

**For the garnishing**

2 tsp coconut slices, fried in ghee

**Method**

1.  Heat 1 tsp ghee and fry the nuts and the  raisins.

2.  Dissolve jaggery in 1/2 litre of water and bring it to a boil.

3.  Add the jackfruit and continue to cook, stirring continuously and cook till it thickens.

4.  Add ghee, cardamom powder, fried nuts and the raisins, mix  the contents well and cook for two more minutes. Remove it from fire and transfer the contents to a serving dish.

5.  Garnish it with the fried coconut slices.

6.  Serve hot or cold as desired.

119

# *Vazhakka Pazham Halwa*

## *(Ripe Malabar Plantain Halwa)*

### Ingredients

4 ripe malabar plantains
2 cups jaggery, crumbled
1/2 cup ghee
1 tsp cardamom powder
2 tsp mixed nuts, chopped
2 tsp raisins

### For the garnishing

1/2 tsp saffron strands, soaked in 2 tsp hot milk

### Method

1. Peel and steam the plantains for 5 minutes. Mash them thoroughly.

2. Dissolve jaggery in 3 cups of water and bring it to a boil.

3. Add the mashed bananas, mix well and cook till it thickens.

4. Add ghee, cardamom powder and cook for 2 more minutes.

5. Fry nuts and raisins in 1 tsp ghee and add to the halwa and mix well. Remove it from the fire and transfer the contents to a serving dish.

6. Pour the saffron milk over the halwa.

7. Serve hot or cold as desired.

# Vazhakka Pazham Uniappam

## (Banana-n-Rice Moulds)

**Ingredients**
3 cups rice flour
2 cups jaggery, crumbled
2 ripe malabar plantains
1/2 tsp freshly grated coconut
1/2 tsp cardamom powder
1/2 tsp baking soda
coconut oil for frying

**For the garnishing**
1/2 cup mixed nuts, grated

**Method**
1.  Wash, peel and chop the plantains.
2.  Boil 2 cups of water and dissolve jaggery in it.
3.  Add coconut, cardamom powder to it and boil the syrup till it reaches a thick consistency.
4.  Mix the rice flour, the banana and the baking soda till well combined.
5.  Add syrup to the flour mixture and knead to a smooth dough.
6.  Fill the uniappam moulds with the prepared dough and fry in oil along with the mould.
7.  Remove the appams from the mould and transfer it to a serving plate.
8.  Garnish it with the grated nuts.
9.  Serve hot.

# Appam

## (Rice-n-Jaggery Delicacy)

### Ingredients

2 1/2 cups rice
2 cups jaggery, crumbled
1 coconut, grated
1 tsp pepper powder
coconut oil for frying

### Method

1. Soak the rice for two hours and grind it coarsely.

2. Add jaggery and grind it to a smooth paste.

3. Add required quantity of water to the paste and make a thick batter.

4. Mix the batter, pepper powder and the grated coconut till well combined.

5. Heat oil in a frying pan and pour a spoonful of batter into it. Fry till golden. Drain well.

6. Serve hot.

# Achchappam

## (Rose Cookies)

### Ingredients

4 cups rice
1/4 litre milk
2 cups powdered sugar
3 eggs
1 tsp cardamom powder
coconut oil for frying

## Method

1. 'Wash and soak the rice for two hours.

2. Grind the rice with milk to a thick batter.

3. Beat the eggs thoroughly and add to the batter along with sugar and the cardamom powder. Mix well.

4. Heat oil in a pan and dip the achchappam mould in it for a minute.

5. Dip the mould into the batter and then dip it in the hot oil. Fry along with the mould. Tap the mould for the appam to separate. Repeat the same till the batter is over.

6. This sweet can be preserved for a week.

# Kumbilappam
## (Steamed Fruit Cones)

123

### Ingredients

1 cup ripe jackfruit pulp or mango pulp
1 cup rice flour, slightly roasted
1 cup jaggery, crumbled
1 cup freshly grated coconut
1/4 tsp salt
1/4 tsp cardamom powder
1/4 tsp cinnamon powder
1/4 tsp nutmeg powder

### For the topping

Coconut oil or ghee or sweet (thick) coconut milk

### Method

1. Mix all the ingredients till well combined.

2. Make small cones with the banana leaves which are greased with ghee or coconut oil.

3. Fill the cones with the prepared mixture.

4. Seal the cone opening with toothpicks.

5. Steam for 10 minutes.

6. Place the fruit cones on a serving plate and top it with coconut oil or ghee or sweet (thick) coconut milk.

7. Serve hot or cold as desired.

# Ellada

## (Coconut-n-Jaggery Delight)

**Ingredients**
2 cups rice flour
2 cups freshly grated coconut
2 cups jaggery, crumbled
4 tsp mixed nuts, grated
1 tsp cardamom powder
1/4 tsp salt

**For the topping**
Ghee or sweet (thick) coconut milk

**Method**

1. Dissolve jaggery in two cups of water and boil over low heat for about 5 minutes.

2. Add grated coconut, cardamom powder and the grated nuts. Boil till the contents are thick and nearly dry.

3. Roast the rice flour slightly and allow it to cool.

4. Mix the rice flour and the salt till well combined and add 1/2 cup of water to it. Mix the contents well and knead it to a smooth dough.

5. Divide the dough and the coconut filling into equal portions.

6. Press a dough ball on a greased banana leaf into a round shape as thin as possible.

7. Place the filling on one half and gently fold the banana leaf. Repeat the same till the dough and the filling are over.

8. Steam the elladas for 10 minutes.

9. Serve with a dollop of ghee spooned over it or spoon sweet coconut milk on the elladas and serve.

# Sukhiyan
## (Whole Green Gram Delight)

**Ingredients**
2 cups maida
1/2 tsp salt

**For the filling**
1 cup whole green gram (whole moong dal)
1 cup jaggery, crumbled
1 tsp cardamom powder
1 tsp freshly grated coconut
Coconut oil for frying

**Method**
1. Mix the maida, salt and the required amount of water and make a thick batter.

2. Cook the whole moong till just tender in water and drain.

3. Mix the cooked moong, jaggery, cardamom powder and the grated coconut till well combined.

4. Shape the filling into round balls.

5. Dip the balls in the maida batter and fry in hot oil till light brown. Drain well.

6. Serve hot or cold as desired.

125

# Aval Vilayichathu

## (Beaten Rice Delicacy)

### Ingredients
500 gm beaten rice (poha)
500 gm jaggery, crumble
1/2 cup sesame seeds
1/2 cup moong dal
1 tsp cardamom powder
1 coconut, grated
1 tsp cumin seeds
1/2 tsp dry ginger powder
1 cup ghee

### Method
1. Roast the sesame and the cumin seeds.

2. Heat ghee and fry the beaten rice till crisp. Drain well.

3. Dissolve jaggery in 4 cups of water and bring it to boil for 5 minutes.

4. Add grated coconut and cook till the coconut is tender.

5. Add the roasted seeds, cardamom powder, dry ginger powder, mix the contents well and cook till the contents thicken. Remove from the fire.

6. In the meantime, soak the moong dal for 2 hours and drain. Fry in ghee till golden. Add to the jaggery mixture along with the fried beaten rice. Mix the contents well.

   Shape the mixture into lemon sized balls. This can be stored for a week in air-tight tins.

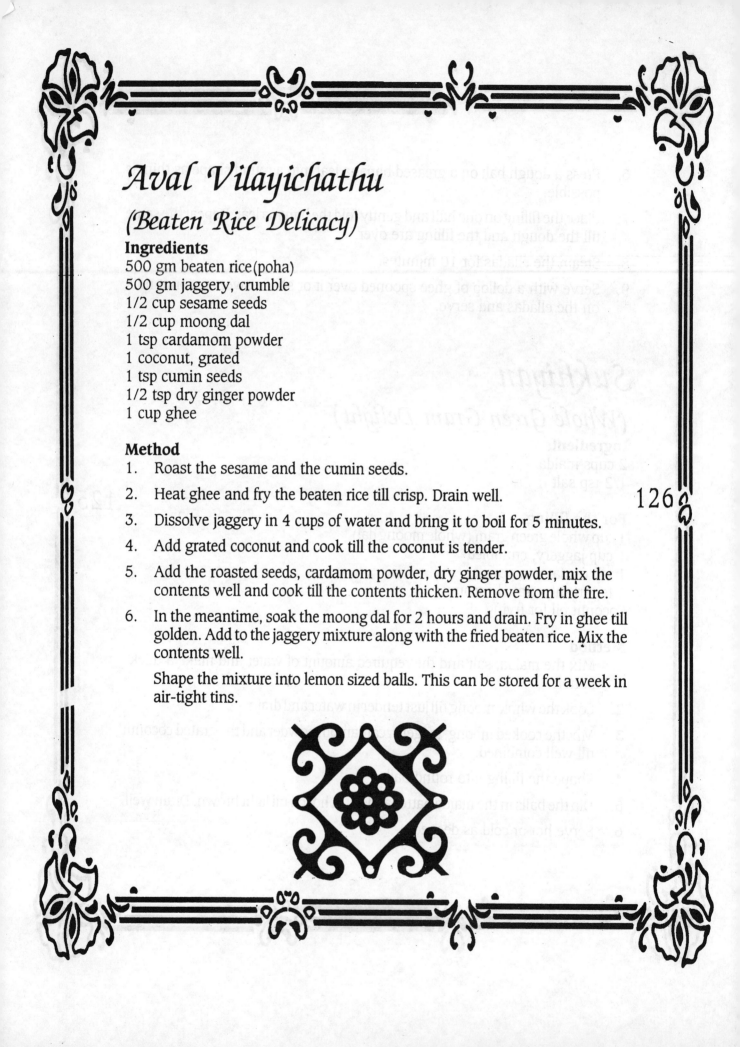

# Kozhikatta

## (Rice Balls in Coconut Milk)

**Ingredients**

2 cups rice flour
1 coconut, grated
1 tsp cardamom powder
2 tsp ghee
A pinch of salt
1 cup sugar

**For the garnishing**

4 tsp mixed nuts, grated

**Method**

1.  Roast the rice flour till the raw smell disappears.

2.  Add rice flour, ghee and the salt to 4 cups of water and bring the contents to boil. When it forms lumps, remove from the fire and shape into lemon size balls.

3.  Extract coconut milk by adding 2 cups of warm water to the grated coconut.

4.  Disslove sugar in the coconut milk and bring to a boil.

5.  Add the rice balls, and the cardamom powder. Cook for 5 minutes, turning the balls. Remove from the fire and transfer the contents to a serving dish.

6.  Sprinkle grated nuts on the dish.

7.  Serve hot or cold as desired.

# Churuttu

## *(Stuffed Rice Delicacy)*

**Ingredients**

**For the dough**
4 cups rice flour

**For the filling**
4 cups rice flour
2 coconuts, grated
2 tsp cumin seeds
1/2 kg sugar

**Method**

1. Sieve and sift the rice flour into a bowl. Add to it the required quantity of warm water and knead it to a smooth dough.

2. Roast the rice flour for the filling till light brown.

3. Mix the roasted rice flour, grated coconut and the cumin seeds till well combined.

4. Dissolve sugar in 1/2 litre of water and bring it to a boil till it reaches thick syrup consistency.

5. Add the prepared filling, mix the contents thoroughly and remove from the fire.

6. Divide the dough and the filling into equal portions.

7. Spread one dough ball on the floured board as thin as possible to a round shape. Toast it on a greased tava till cooked on either side. Repeat the same till the dough balls are over.

8. Shape the rice chapati into a cone and fill it with the prepared filling.

9. Spoon ghee over it and serve.

# Diamond Cuts

**Ingredients**
250 gm maida
2 cups sugar
Ghee or coconut oil for frying

**For the garnishing**
1/2 cup freshly grated coconut
1 tsp cardamom powder

**Method**
1. Sieve and make a soft dough with maida with the required quantity of water.

2. Divide the dough into lemon sized balls.

3. Roll the dough balls on the floured board as thin as possible into a round shape. Cut the rolled out dough into diamond shape.

4. Fry them in ghee or coconut oil till crisp.

5. Dissolve sugar in 2 cups of water and bring to a boil. Make a thick sugar syrup.

6. Drop the diamond pieces into the syrup and thoroughly coat it on all sides.

7. Place the diamonds in a serving plate and sprinkle freshly grated coconut and cardamom powder on them.

8. Serve as a tea-time delicacy.

# Vazhakka Pazham Porichadhu

## (Ripe Malabar Plantain Fritters)

### Ingredients
2 Malabar ripe plantain
2 cups maida
2 tsp rice flour
1/4 tsp salt
1 cup sugar

### For the garnishing
2 tsp grated and roasted coconut
2 tsp grated nuts

### Method
1. Peel and slice the plantains into 3 pieces.

2. Cut each piece lengthwise into 4 pieces.

3. Mix maida, salt and sugar with enough water and make a thick batter.

4. Dip the plantain pieces in the batter and fry in oil till crisp. Drain well.

5. Place the banana fritters on a serving plate and sprinkle grated and roasted coconut and nuts on it.

6. Serve at tea-time.

130

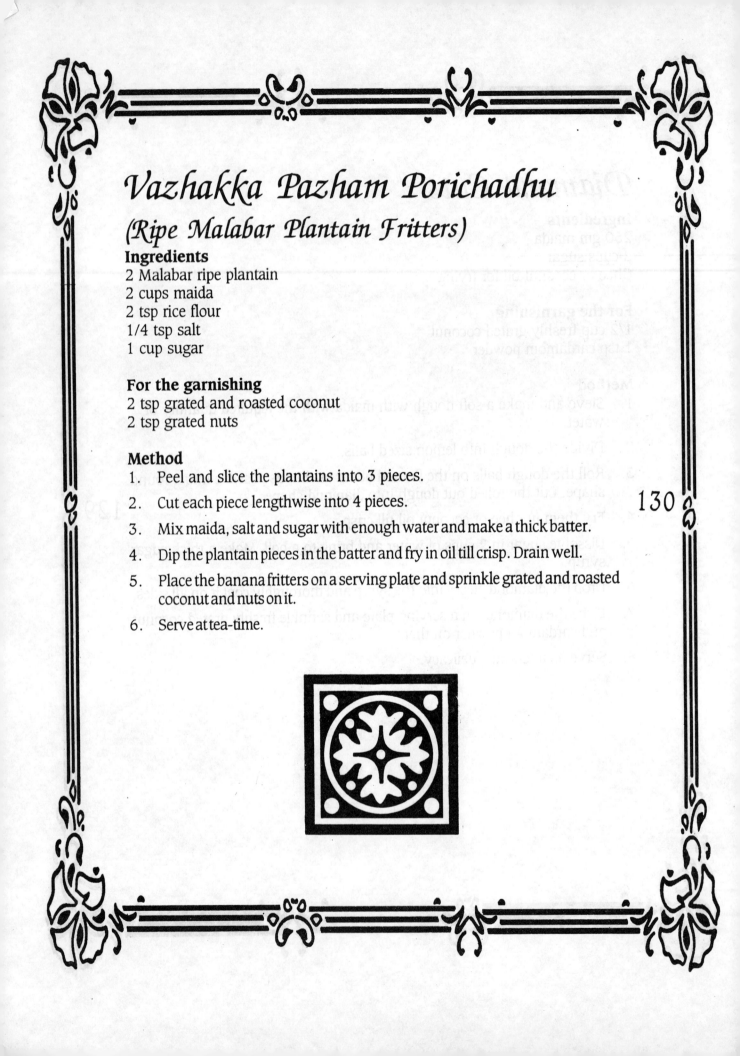

# Chakka Pazham Porichadhu

## (Ripe Jackfruit Fritters)

### Ingredients
2 cups ripe jackfruit, minced'
1 cup freshly grated coconut
2 cups maida
1/4 tsp salt
2 cups sugar
1 egg, beaten thoroughly
Coconut oil for frying

### For the garnshing
2 tsp grated and roasted coconut
2 tsp grated nuts

### Method
1.  Add one cup of warm water to the grated coconut and extract the coconut milk.

2.  Mix the extract milk, minced jackfruit, maida, salt, sugar and the beaten egg till well combined, so as to form a thick batter.

3.  Heat oil and pour spoonfull of batter into it. Fry till crisp and golden. Drain well.

4.  Transfer the contents to a serving plate and garnish it with the roasted coconut and the green nuts.

# Elainchi

## (Sweet Pancake)

**Ingredients**
**For the batter**
500 gm maida
1 egg, beaten thoroughly
1 tsp salt

**For the filling**
1 cup beaten rice
1 cup powdered sugar
1 cup freshly grated coconut
1 tsp cardamom powder
1/2 cup milk

**Method**

1. Mix all the filling ingredients till well combined.

2. Mix maida, beaten egg and the salt alongwith enough quantity of water so as to form a loose batter.

3. Spread a big spoonfull of batter on a greased tava and spread little filling over it. Roll it.

4. Repeat the same till the batter and the filling is over.

5. Spoon coconut oil over the pancke.

6. Serve hot.